THE COMMON GLORY

Old Jamestown, site of the first permanent English settlement in the new world, a hallowed spot in American history and the inspiration of our dreams. (*Virginia State Chamber of Commerce*)

Thomas Jefferson (played by Walter Brooke) writing the Declaration of Independence, Act I, Scene 6. (*Colonial Studios*)

THE COMMON GLORY

A Symphonic Drama of American History

WITH MUSIC, COMMENTARY,
ENGLISH FOLKSONG AND DANCE

PAUL GREEN

Published for THE JAMESTOWN CORPORATION
and VIRGINIA CONSERVATION COMMISSION

By The University of North Carolina Press
CHAPEL HILL

Copyright, 1948, by Paul Green

Printed in the United States of America
The Van Rees Press, NEW YORK

P. J.

To

COLGATE W. DARDEN, JR.

In Appreciation

Author's Note

By symphonic drama I mean that type of drama in which all elements of theatre art are used to sound together—one for all and all for one, a true democracy. The theatre of such a drama is sensitized and charged with a fierce potential of evocation and expressiveness for any moment.

A charmed circle it is. He who enters there may well consider that he is entering the ritual of a zealous priesthood and his prerogative is to fit the freedom of his own individual and undogmatic self as creator into it.

It is not vice-versa.

All tokens of statement and outward give and take and intensification are incorporated and available here for the dramatic artist's needs—poetry, dance pantomime, mental speech, masks, choreography, story-line, song and music. These are indeed the elements of this drama and its theatre.

And always there is music—music!

Time is telescoped here through a symbol—and becomes that symbol. So with space. Compress it or expand it at your will like the breathing, say, of some huge and delicate accordion of the mind!

It is a theatre free as a dream in its self-creativeness. And its methodology and technique are finally sufficient for all requirements and challenges of the imagination.

It is the imagination we now lack—the imagination unbound!

P.G.

"... and finally, that truth is great and will prevail if left to herself; that she is the proper and sufficient antagonism to error, and has nothing to fear from the conflict unless by human interpretation disarmed of her natural weapons, free argument and debate; errors ceasing to be dangerous when it is permitted freely to contradict them."

—JEFFERSON'S BILL FOR ESTABLISHING RELIGIOUS FREEDOM, 1779

THE COMMON GLORY

TIME

The latter part of the eighteenth century

PLACE

England and America

Act I

Scene 1: Prologue
Scene 2: The palace of King George the Third in London, summer, 1775
Scene 3: The house of burgesses in Williamsburg, Virginia, May, 1776
Scene 4: Before the gaol in Williamsburg, some days later
Scene 5: The garden of Robert Gordon's house in Williamsburg, night of the same day
Scene 6: A rooming-house in Philadelphia, summer, several weeks later
Scene 7: The palace green in Williamsburg, some weeks later

Act II

Scene 1: A Virginia montage sequence, two years later
Scene 2: An inner office in the governor's palace in Williamsburg, autumn, 1779
Scene 3: A committee room in the capitol in Williamsburg, a short time later
Scene 4: The ruined churchyard at Jamestown, a winter night, 1780
Scene 5: An inner council room in the palace of King George the Third, some months later
Scene 6: The battlefield at Yorktown, October, 1781
Scene 7: A farmhouse near Yorktown, a few days later
Scene 8: The bluffs of Richmond, sometime later

CHARACTERS

(In the order of their appearance)

The Narrator
Two Trumpeters
A Court Dancer
A Major-domo
A British Flag-bearer
King George III, *ruler of England*
Lord North, *his prime minister*
The Spanish Ambassador
The French Ambassador
Lord Cornwallis
Robert Gordon, *a Tory leader in Virginia*
Eileen Gordon, *his daughter*
William Pitt, *the English liberal leader and former prime minister*
A Messenger
Samuel Adams ⎫
Edmund Pendleton ⎪
Richard Bland ⎪
Paul Carrington ⎪
Archibald Cary ⎬ *members of the Virginia Convention of 1776*
Bartholomew Dandridge ⎪
Dudley Digges ⎪
Benjamin Harrison ⎪
Patrick Henry ⎪
Thomas Jefferson ⎭

CHARACTERS

Richard Henry Lee
Thomas Ludwell Lee
James Madison
George Mason
Thomas Nelson
Robert Carter Nicholas } *members of the Virginia Convention of 1776*
Mann Page
Edmund Randolph
Champion Travis
George Wythe

Cephus Sicklemore, *a man of words and no property*
Peter Pelham, *a musician and keeper of the Williamsburg gaol*
Mammy Huzzitt, *a hardworking Williamsburg widow*
Hugh Taylor, *a young frontiersman and patriot*
Sarah Hallam, *a Williamsburg beauty and actress*
The Town Crier
Sergeant Jack, *of the Virginia Militia*
The Huzzitt Children
Maria Byrd, *wife of Colonel William Byrd*
Francis Corbin, *a young Virginia aristocrat in love with Eileen*

Mr. Ambler
Mr. Bucktrout
Mr. Burwell
Colonel Corbin
Dr. Camm } *loyalist sympathizers*
Mr. Carpenter
Mr. Hill
Mr. Ross
Mr. Sprowle
Mr. Wormley

CHARACTERS

Benjamin Franklin
John Adams
Roger Sherman
Robert Livingston
Patty Jefferson, *wife of Thomas Jefferson*
Reverend Mr. Madison, *of the College of William and Mary*
An American Flag-bearer
A Boy Clerk
A Patriot Captain
Martha Carr, *Jefferson's sister*
The Carr Children
Martha, *Jefferson's little daughter*
Aunt Nancy, *Patty Jefferson's old slave nurse*
First Legislator
Second Legislator
Third Legislator
Fourth Legislator
The Figure of Death
The Ghost of John Smith
The Ghost of John Rolfe
The Ghost of Nathaniel Bacon
The Ghost of Pocahontas
General George Washington
Lieutenant-Colonel Alexander Hamilton
General Lafayette
Count de Rochambeau
General Steuben
A Hessian Soldier

also

Lords at the Court
Ladies at the Court
Courtiers

CHARACTERS

Dancing Girls
Members of the Virginia Convention
Six Williamsburg Girls
American Soldiers
British Soldiers
Indians
Negro Slaves and Servants
Farmers
Convicts
Guards
Townspeople of Williamsburg
Children

Act One

SCENE 1

It is the twilight hour, and the audience is gathered in the outdoor theatre for the play. As the shadows deepen down the glen and the stars begin to shine in the misty mirror of the little lake beyond the stage, an organ starts playing an overture in praise of God and nature and great men dead and gone—at first a grand crash of chords and rumbling mass of sound suggestive of energy and war and the turmoiling of men's souls and bodies—followed by a harmony more thoughtful, meditative and lofty.

The music moves its way forward in a great wind of harmony which permeates and suffuses the woods now

in its own manner as the noiseless-footed twilight has begun to do. The lights slowly die down in the theatre and a spot holds on the organist up and behind the left side stage, illuminating him in a circle of brightness as he inserts a sprightly twinkling dance.

The little dance twists and turns and develops merrily, and then the music goes back to the grave pomp of the mighty hymn. This is the signal for the chorus which begins assembling in the darkness on the front center stage. The light fades down on the organist and rises in a nebulous glow on the chorus standing in front of the now closed woodland hedge curtain and behind the footlights. The chorus consists of some twenty or thirty young men and women and all dressed in neutral-patterned garments and made up with full-dimensioned mouths so as to emphasize their function as sources of song—but not comically so. Framing the group of singers on either side are two tall soldiers in splendid uniform and at shoulder arms. The one on the left is British, the one on the right American.

The organ builds to a climax of reverberating chords and stops. For an instant there is silence. A low chord is struck by the organist in the darkness. The chorus begins a gentle and wordless harmony which seems at first like the wandering vast and murmuring wind among the woodland trees. It gradually strengthens into an affirmation of words—clear and distinct in the growing tide of harmony.

Chorus

Out of the rich and deep-bosomed earth,
Mother of all, life-giving and bountiful,
Thou builder and thou leveler,
For thee these words!
(*The organ makes a commenting swirl of music, moving into another mood. The chorus is carried along with it, now declaring a sudden and almost stern interrogation.*)
Deep in the tomb is there no voice now,
Here by the low enclosing wall of quiet,
Silent in the evening's grievous hush!
(*Now plaintively.*)
All muted is the fresh up-flaming morn,
All tongueless waits the lordly mountain top.
(*Almost fiercely.*)
Shall these souls be bound in
The tremulous chains of the starlight,
Or dust and ashes befoul
The bright head of beauty!
(*In loud lament.*)

O fading footsteps lost forever,
O eloquent lips, the passionate hearts
And gesturing final hands!

(For a moment the chorus holds its final threnodic chord. The lights fade down, and both the soldiers and the chorus turn about-face and stand hid in shadow. A glow comes up on the side stage at the right. The narrator of the play comes through the proscenium door and stands on this little stage. A spot from the light tower now brilliantly illuminates him. He is an elderly clean-shaven man with a kindly face and deep pleasant voice and dressed in eighteenth century costume—knee breeches, powdered wig, gleaming shoe buckles and velvet coat. He might be a prideful old time colonial school teacher or even an elderly George Wythe himself, professor of law at the College of William and Mary. He carries a silver-headed cane in his hand with grace and elegance, and stands looking out over the audience.)

Narrator

Friends, we are gathered here this evening to do honor to our forefathers—the men who laid the mighty foundations of this government under which we live today. And it is fitting that we have chosen this place for our celebration.

(Gesturing inclusively in the air.)

This nook of Virginia lying between the York and James Rivers is indeed the birthplace of the republic and likewise the cradle of its liberty.

(Nodding toward the right.)

There, just over the hill at Jamestown, occurred the immortal tragedy of suffering and death—the birth pangs of

a nation's creation nearly three hundred and fifty years ago. And here at Williamsburg in the eighteenth century—
(*Gesturing again.*)
—were rived out and developed most of the matchless documents and statements of liberty upon which our self-government has been builded.
(*Now nodding in front of him.*)
And just over there at Yorktown in 1781 the victory was finally won which made us an independent people.
(*After an instant of pause.*)
This is indeed sacred soil whereon we are gathered tonight.
(*His voice deepening.*)
Here where I stand at this moment—from time immemorial the elusive deer have trod,, and the flitting light-winged bird! And the tripping tender maid, Pocahontas herself, has walked here. Down the trail that leads through this very amphitheatre prideful old Powhatan, Emperor of the Western World, and his warriors have marched to battle. Here the glamorous John Smith and the devout John Rolfe and Sir Thomas Dale of the hard heart and the iron hand—and the rash, and magnificent Nathaniel Bacon—all have passed this way.
(*His voice lifting lyrically.*)
The very leaves of the trees whereunder we sit at this hour have trembled to the eloquence of the dramatic Patrick Henry.
(*He gestures slightly to the right.*)
There where the path crosses our stage, the youthful Thomas Jefferson has walked on many a summer or autumn evening, musing and thinking and watching the sunset sky, the deepful upper air and the stars above, making his notes in his little book and dreaming his dreams. Yes, dreaming his dreams.

(*Gesturing inclusively again.*)
Here in Virginia has been the breeding place of great men.
　(*Fervently.*)
God grant that we remember them!
God grant that their sacrifice remain like a bright flame
Forever burning and pure in our hearts!
　(*He lowers his head and turns indicatingly toward the chorus. The light dies from him, and unseen by the audience he moves away into the darkness and takes his place in the narrator's box up and behind the side stage much in the same position as the organist on the opposite side of the theatre. The light comes up as before on the center stage, and the two soldiers and the chorus make their military about-face toward the audience.*)

CHORUS

(*Chanting.*)
Here in the silence of these hills
The earliest footfall, the morning and evening voice
The startled cry, the halloo of the waking man,
The green branch and the shoot of the floods declining,
The bird song and the rising light
Of the new day dawning!
Hail to thee,
Hail to thy sons heroic
Spirit unconquerable!

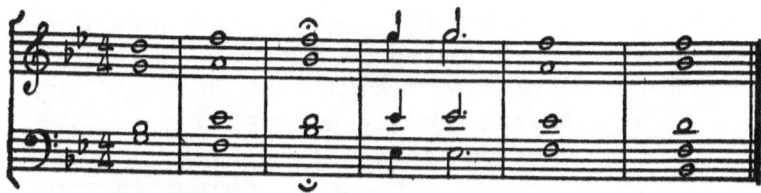

Sing, sing, sing,
All hail, hail, hail!
(*The light fades from the chorus and comes up on the narrator's niche or box.*)

NARRATOR

(*Speaking above his book, his amplified voice moving out across the night.*)
In the latter part of the eighteenth century when George the Third ascended the throne of Britain the cause of liberty in the world received a serious blow. Perverse and selfish and obstinate, this king laid the tyranny of his heavy hand upon the American colonies. He conceived of them as children, and as such they must obey his will—and for his own pleasure and profit. If he needed taxes they must pay them. If he wanted their trade, they must give it. If they deserved punishment, he would send his soldiers to administer it.

Protesting, petitioning, and pleading in vain, the colonies finally rose in rebellion. At Lexington on April 19, 1775, a band of New England patriots met the king's forces in battle. The Revolutionary War had begun—a war that was to change the ways of men's thinking as no war has before or since—as we shall see.

The more liberal-minded men in England—and there were some still left—heard the news of this bloodshed with horror. Among them was the great commoner, William Pitt. Rising from a bed of desperate illness, he drove through the night to London to plead once more with the stubborn king. His majesty's courtiers and their ladies were in victorious mood that night—and had assembled at the palace to celebrate with music and fun.

(*The light fades from the narrator and comes up in two spots on the forestage. Two young trumpeters come in from the right and left, carrying trumpets held in front of them. They are dressed in satin and lace and silver-buckled shoes that gleam and sparkle in the light. They stand in the spots and blow a long flourish—sounded in the organ.*)

(*As if in rhythm to their blowing, the hedge curtain divides and slides back behind the proscenium walls to the right and left. The light comes up on the center stage showing the scene in a blaze of glory. The two trumpeters turn back the way they came and stop by the stage tormentors in the shadow.*)

SCENE 2

The resplendent audience chamber in the palace of King George the Third. At the left rear and set diagonally toward the front is a dais, and on it a sort of throne chair made prominent by a wide gilded panel of framing behind it. A blue silken coverlet is thrown over the chair. Extending out from the shadows at the far left rear of the stage and behind the panel is a terrace wall about waist-high. It is as if the throne room opened out onto an extending stone balcony or second-storey promenade. Set along the promenade are two or three large vases filled with overflowing luxuriant red roses. The scene is gorgeous and colorful.

When the light comes up on the scene, a group of glittering courtiers and ladies-in-waiting and hangers-on around the throne are gathered over at the rear, left. They are representative of a typical cross-section of high and empty English social life and are dressed in the height of fashion—powdered wigs, jewelry, fans, lace, brocade. They are all standing and gazing off to the right. Their faces are lifted and their hands wiggling their handkerchiefs or fans in the air in front of them. The two trumpeters go up and take their place behind the throne chair. In the nearby street beyond the wall we hear the people cheering.

PEOPLE

Long live his majesty! Long live the king!
(Now and then in the distance we hear great guns booming—sounded by the organ. The people in the

18   THE COMMON GLORY

distance begin to sing half-indistinctly, the organ giving the starting chord.)

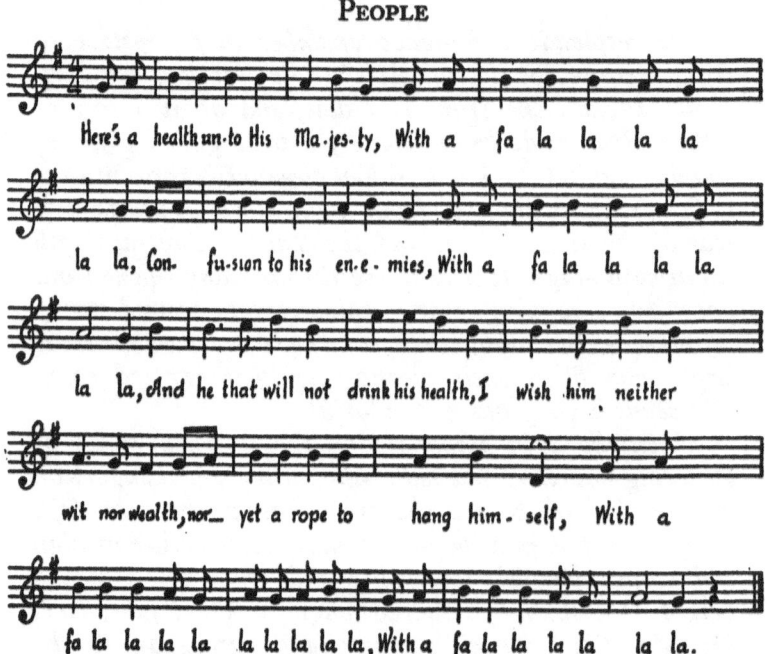

PEOPLE

Here's a health un-to His Ma-jes-ty, With a fa la la la la la la, Con-fu-sion to his en-e-mies, With a fa la la la la la la, And he that will not drink his health, I wish him neither wit nor wealth, nor yet a rope to hang him-self, With a fa la la la la la la la la la, With a fa la la la la la la.

Suddenly a queer little creature about three feet high carrying a tiny wand and wearing the mask of a woodland goblin comes scampering in from the left. He flings up his smallish hands and leads the laughing and cheering courtiers and ladies-in-waiting into the song which is being sung in the distance. The organ now accompanies full-voiced under it. They wind up with a good burst of harmony, and the little dwarf scampers out at the left rear with little whickers of gleeful laughter. And now stepping swiftly in from the right rear and carrying *a large sparkling-headed wand comes the heavy-paunched and bravura major-domo of the king's establishment. He is dressed in a great splurge of scarlet and blue and black and shining silver buckles. A huge order of merit is fastened on his left bosom, giving forth like his wand bright diamond points of scintillation. Accompanying him is a flag-bearer who stops motionless near the throne and stands holding his great banner of scarlet and gold aloft as if in protection over it.*

MAJOR-DOMO

(*In a bellowing voice of announcement.*)
His majesty the king!
(*The trumpeters blow a flourish, followed by a distant booming of guns—all sounded in the organ. The organ now strikes up an ushering march.*)

The gentlemen step back and bow far forward, their hands held outward and down to either side of them in an attitude of deep respect. The women move back and fall on their knees. They begin waving their handkerchiefs, their little fans going. The major-domo straight-

ens up ready to lead the procession of the king and his immediate councillors when they enter. After a moment of expectancy the king enters from the right front. He is followed by a few privy councilors, among them his rubicund minister, Lord North. Orders of merit, jewelry and badges of the king's favor adorn the bosoms of these prime favorites. As the organ plays, the majordomo comes forward and leads the march across the scene. The organ's pride becomes their pride, and the movement is a sort of train of triumph in the big room. King George the Third is as one might gather from his appearance, a softish, kind-hearted, bull-headed man just under forty. There is something womanlike in him too—in his full lips, his plump face, his big and liquid glancing eyes. And yet these eyes, as we soon shall learn, can be steady and hard enough at times. He is dressed in rare color and richness and with touches of jewelry on his person. He lifts his fatty, white, be-ringed hands in a wide and generous greeting to his subjects as they bow before him. His attitude is that of one dispensing the largess of abundant good will, much as he might imagine God himself would do. He makes a sort of grand sweep of the stage, passing across from right to left, then to the left rear and over toward the throne chair. As he approaches the chair the two trumpeters, as if in mutual rhythm and with gestures exactly alike, lean over and smooth the silken pillow in the chair for the approaching kingly bottom. They straighten up again and stand for the remainder of the scene like the flag-bearer, as motionless as two dummies, holding their trumpets by their sides. King George stands in front of the throne, his head thrown back, his face smiling, his highly-dressed wig glistening in the light. He is in fine animal and moral spirits and shows it. The music finishes with a triumphant last chord.

Courtiers

(*Men and women, applauding.*)
Long live our king!
Health and happiness unto you!
God save his majesty!
(*From below and beyond the wall at the back there comes up another cheer of the people. Lord North gestures slightly, and the king steps briskly to the parapet, North behind him. He holds out his hands above the unseen people. The cheers come up again, a surging surfbeat of human sound. The ever-watchful North gathers up an armful of roses from the vases, and hands them to his majesty who holds them aloft and lets them fall to the people below—with the gesture of a man feeding a hungry multitude. The major-domo now shoos the courtiers and ladies back into two wings sweeping away from the center. George returns to the throne and stands in full emblazoned glory before them.*)

King George

(*With real emotion.*)
Bless you, my people! Bless you.

Courtiers

(*All, as they straighten up.*)
Heaven bless you, your majesty!
Bless you! Bless you!

King George

You touch me to the quick with your dear love. And woman's weakness—water drops spill in my eyes—as our poet says.

(*He indeed is deeply touched by the show of affection and respect of his people. With an almost ladyish gesture he puts a lace handkerchief to his face. The people grow suddenly stilled at the tenderheartedness of their monarch. But the brash majordomo turns and walks toward the throne. He has work to do. He turns about-face most militarily and waits beside the monarch's person. George wipes his eyes and controls his voice as he speaks.*)
How sweet the love of my people! In it I find my triumph and my justification. It makes me able to bear these heavy responsibilities. Thus may it always be. And it will! It will!

Voices

(*Half-hushed in respectful emotion.*)
Yes, your majesty. Yes.

King George

(*His brow becoming sultry with spontaneous and rising anger.*)
But some there are, three thousand miles away in America who have not believed my words.
(*Striking his fists together.*)
They are mad. And at Lexington and Concord in the north they have met our arms—
(*Impressively.*)
—and have been destroyed!
(*With a sudden wild cry.*)
Long live England!

People

(*Roaring.*)
England! England! The king! The king!

(*George stretches out his arms once more showing all of the magnificence of his costume and figure and sinks gently back into the throne chair. He exhales a great sigh as if luxuriating in a well-deserved rest after so much labor, so much endeavor undertaken and done. He looks up at the major-domo and nods. The major-domo stalks long-leggedly toward the center front, takes his stance and bawls out over the scene.*)

Major-domo

His excellency—the ambassador of Spain!
(*There is loud applause and a flourish in the organ. The Spanish ambassador enters from the right front. He is a dark, short, pot-bellied man, dressed in the top of fashion. Medals and decorations flare from his breast. He moves toward the king with unction and eagerness and bows low before him. He carries a jewel box held in front of him.*)

Spanish Ambassador

(*With a trace of accent.*)
Your majesty, the high and mighty king of Spain and her possessions—by power of God—presents these jewels in honor of your great victory over your enemies.
(*The king takes the box. He is pleased as a boy with what he sees.*)

King George

(*Jubilantly.*)
Welcome—most welcome.
(*The Spanish ambassador bows again and steps aside. George now has a ring out from the box, puts it on his finger and looks at it admiringly.*)

Major-domo

His excellency—the ambassador of France!
> (*Again there is applause and a louder flourish in the organ. The French ambassador enters. He is typical, gracious and swift-moving, and carries a roll of foolscap parchment tied with a ribbon. He bows low before the king.*)

French Ambassador

> (*Also with an accent.*)

I bring greetings from his most Christian and sovereign king of France, by grace of God. Signed with his own sacred hand, this document doth witness again the peace and friendship between our two great peoples—honoring thy victorious arms.
> (*The king takes the parchment.*)

King George

> (*Jubilantly.*)

We will make courteous and fitting reply to these great honors and trusts—
> (*Pointedly to Lord North.*)

—by royal messenger.

Lord North

> (*Nodding.*)

We shall at once, your majesty.

Major-domo

> (*Bawling again.*)

The Earl of Cornwallis!—
> (*There is a flourish in the organ, and the people applaud as Cornwallis enters, followed by Robert Gordon and his daughter Eileen.*)

—and his guests from Virginia!
(*Cornwallis is a stout forthright soldier of middle-age and wears a sword at his side. Gordon is a handsomely dressed Virginia councilman. He is about fifty years old and of almost granite-like dignity and strength of character. His daughter Eileen is about twenty, like her father dressed in the height of fashion, and very beautiful. She carries a handsomely bound volume on a satin pillow held before her.*)

Voices

(*Ad lib.*)
From Virginia. You hear that.

Cornwallis

My humble greetings, your majesty.

King George

Most welcome to my presence, my Lord Cornwallis.

Cornwallis

(*Leading Gordon forward.*)
I present your most loyal servant and councilman from Williamsburg, Virginia—my friend Robert Gordon and his daughter Eileen.

King George

(*Heartily reciting his rote.*)
Welcome, welcome, most worthy councilor.

Gordon

(*As he bows before the king.*)
Your majesty.

(*The king with a wide pleased smile of admiration extends his hand to Eileen. She comes forward and curtsies, prideful and self-possessed.*)

King George

I reward your beauty, my dear. You may kiss my hand. (*Gordon takes the pillow with its book from her. She bends and kisses his majesty's hand.*)

Cornwallis

(*Indicating Gordon.*)
Recently come to London on business, he sails again soon for Virginia.

Gordon

(*His voice strong, certain.*)
I bring greetings, sire, from your most ancient colony Virginia—firm in her loyalty to your person and the crown and glory of England!

King George

(*Joyously.*)
We have never doubted the loyalty of our oldest dominion.

Voices

(*Loudly, cheering.*)
Virginia! Virginia!

Gordon

True there have been a few traitorous spirits there. But the notorious Patrick Henry has now been banished the capital by decree of Governor Dunmore. And—
(*Impressively and sternly.*)
the radical Thomas Jefferson—unhappily a kinsman of mine—has returned to the mountains to the west—his home. Warships ride in the rivers nearby, and English

marines parade the streets of Williamsburg. The power of your majesty's arms and the devotion of your loyal people there will keep that domain safe for England—
(*Turning toward the courtiers.*)
—a domain vast as all colonies else combined—stretching from the Atlantic Ocean to the Mississippi River on the west and to the Great Lakes on the north.

King George

(*His eyes shining.*)
My heart is humble in thankfulness this day. Ah, my Lord Cornwallis.

Cornwallis

Your majesty.

Gordon

Herewith I tender your majesty this book of greetings —inscribed therein by the honorable governor and his council, and the planters, merchants, burgesses throughout the colony—from Richmond, Fredericksburg, Petersburg, Hampton, Portsmouth, Norfolk, Williamsburg, Yorktown.
(*The king listens attentively to the roll of names.*)

King George

Of Yorktown I have not heard.

Gordon

A humble place, your majesty, but I am convinced of great military importance.
(*He holds the pillow out and the king lifts the book from it. He examines it delightedly, kisses it, and lays it back. North receives the pillow and book from Gordon and passes them on to the second*

trumpeter. The king leans back in his chair with great luxuriance, regarding his people with satisfaction and indulgence. Happiness exudes from his person. Suddenly he springs up.)

King George

(His voice vibrant.)
And thus, my beloved people, secure in the friendship of our two great allies, in the loyalty of the vast dominion of Virginia—in the power of our arms and the righteousness of our cause—England stands triumphant at this hour.
(With a sweeping gesture toward the rear.)
And under that bright banner of empire the oppressed peoples of the earth shall continue to find their guarantees, their refuge and their strength.
(Quickly and piously, his liquid eyes lifted a moment.)
Let us give thanks to Almighty God who has so blest us—amen, amen!
(He sinks back again into his chair.)

People

(Likewise piously.)
Amen.
(The king looks out at the major-domo again and nods.)

Major-domo

And now—music! Music!
(The organ sounds a crash of chords. The little dwarf scampers in again from the left rear. He stops in the middle of the scene, turns and bows in the direction from whence he came. A group of royal

musicians, some eight or ten, enter at the left rear. They stop on the terrace and strike up a joyous English dance and continue—sounded in the organ.)

(*Running in from the left rear and in front of the musicians come some eight or ten young dancing girls in ballet costumes. The king and the people all register their delight. The musicians lighten into a prancing interpretation, and the girls execute their gay turns and swirls before the monarch. As the piece proceeds, the people in the room get infected,*

including the little dwarf who goes jiggling around the flag-bearer. They clap their hands, and some of the courtiers and ladies begin cutting steps where they stand. The dancers now move up to the king, and then begin winging about the throne. George reaches out to grab their little fluttering hands kissingly in passing. He too gets infected by the rhythm and spirit of the moment. Rising from his seat, he starts going it with right good will and impetuosity. The dance builds in fervor. At the climax a loud raucous voice is heard calling in the distance off at the left. The music as if bothered makes a wobble in its rhythm.)

VOICE

Your majesty! Your majesty!
(The king looks quickly away, his steps slowing. Those behind him slow likewise and look off. The flag-bearer and trumpeters continue to stand motionless. The voice is now at hand. It is repeated in the amplification.)
Your majesty!
(Entering at the left front comes old William Pitt, the Earl of Chatham. He is a dark inspiring figure—enveloped in a black and voluminous cape, his long and scraggly white hair topped off by a huge triangular drooping old hat. His face is thin, his nose high and beaklike, and his two cavernous eyes gleam from under his hat with the piercing intentness of a hawk. His feet are crippled and swollen and bandaged, and he walks with the aid of two crutches partly hid in the folds of his cape. The dance suddenly stops and so does the music. The king as if taking refuge from some terrible apparition moves a step or two back toward the throne. The major-

domo *retires to the right front and watches the scene with cold unconcern.*)

PITT

(*Fiercely, angrily.*)
Your majesty!

KING GEORGE

(*Bitingly, after a moment.*)
I was informed my Lord Pitt was fatally ill in bed.
(*Ironically.*)
And yet here he is come to honor our victory day.

PITT

(*His voice trembling.*)
Since you err in the first judgment, my liege, mayhap you likewise do in the second.
(*The king moves farther back toward the throne as if needing its help. The courtiers and dancers and others also move somewhat toward the left and right rear as if feeling the inimical power of the intruder. The musicians at the rear gradually steal off the way they came as the scene proceeds.*)

PITT

(*Scathingly.*)
As always—surrounded by these—
(*With bitter scorn.*)
—these people!
(*He spits out the word "people."*)
Bah! Sycophants, flatterers, blood-suckers around the throne—singing and dancing their country's life away, dabbling in her blood!
(*The courtiers mutter angrily, and the ladies turn away their faces. The king is now back at the*

throne and feels the strength of its proximity. The major-domo shoos the dancers out of the scene at the left rear following the musicians.)

Lord North
(Sharply.)
If the Earl of Chatham would plead a cause, let him do so in private, your majesty.

Pitt
(Ragingly.)
I have no secret. As for these—
(He waves his crutch.)
—empty pates and witless fops—their mouldy brains cannot receive the speech of an honest man.
(Again the courtiers mutter and mumble.)

King George
(Now master of himself again.)
Let this poor misguided old minister condemn himself as he will. My heart is innocent before the waiting world.
(He makes a gesture toward the courtiers indicating them as the world. Pitt takes a few steps toward the throne and stops on his crutches. King George shrinks back a bit, then gazes at him from his eminence on the dais.)
What is your plea, my lord?

Pitt
(His voice hoarse and strident.)
One that the smallest gesture of your lifted hand can grant—prevent the bloody civil war now breaking between this country and the colonies.

King George

(*Easily and stubbornly.*)
So it is being prevented. My decree has gone forth—
(*Loudly.*)
—let all rebels whatsoever lay down their arms, acknowledge their error and take the oath of loyalty to the throne—they must. They shall!

Pitt

(*Swallowing, and keeping control of himself.*)
Is it true that a fleet of ships and soldiers and cannon is now being prepared against our brothers beyond the sea?

King George

(*Calling out confidently.*)
I do confess my weakness in my deep love for England. It is true. They sail tomorrow—against our enemies, not our brothers—
(*Gesturing.*)
—with my Lord Cornwallis aboard.
(*Cornwallis looks up.*)

Pitt

(*With a groan.*)
Then the throne is mad!
(*Turning pleadingly to Cornwallis.*)
I pray you, my Lord Cornwallis, add your great voice to mine, that we may bring his majesty to his senses.

Voices

(*Angrily.*)
Treason!

King George

(*His eyes hardening, his voice chilling.*)
Once again my lord, I warn you—that your former great services to our empire may not always protect you in your insults to your king.

Pitt

I have no fear. Destroy me if you will, seal my lips forever, strangle me in a string on highest Tyburn Hill, but still my last cry shall be the proud voice of a free Englishman.
(*Almost viciously.*)
These rebels as you call them—Washington and Henry, and Adams and Franklin are fighting the fight of free men everywhere—of Englishmen that once walked and lived in this island but now are dead or corrupted—the fight of Milton, of Cromwell, of Locke, of the great Sir Walter Raleigh, of Shakespeare—and of all who have stood for liberty.

Lord North

(*Irritably.*)
You may spare his majesty this stale lesson in history.
(*The growling of the impatient courtiers now increases. Some of them angrily move a little closer to the fanatical Chatham as if to surround him. But his voice snarls and whips through the air and stops them again as the fierce heat of his own burning passion scorches them back.*)

Pitt

Hearken to me—this solemn warning—in the eloquent words of a man all England should be proud to own—
(*With bony trembling and eager hand he has pulled*

out a document from the caverns of his cape and now holds it aloft and shakingly in the air.)
—Thomas Jefferson—
   (*Rushing on.*).
—If another ship is sent against America—
   (*As if quotingly.*)
—"if another hireling soldier puts his foot upon our shores whether in Massachusetts or Georgia"—Hear me!
—"then the colony of Virginia will rise in all her might and hurl her growing thousands of vengeful patriots into the fray until the tyrant's troops are beat back into the sea."

Lord North

(*Loudly.*)
An empty threat, your majesty!
   (*Pitt hobbles forward and pushes the document into the king's hand.*)

Pitt

Read it, your majesty—listen to the voice of reason. Let us delay the sailing of these ships. Let us seek earnestly and with restraint to settle these differences that the blood of brother against brother may not shame us with everlasting disgrace! Let us wait, wait.
   (*The words of the fiery commoner have now begun to make an impression in the room. The king sits silent a moment, staring out before him.*)

King George

(*After a moment, but ironically and with hidden stubbornness.*)
If the noble Lord Cornwallis would deign reply to this ancient and misguided minister—well, you may do so.

LORD NORTH

(*Interposingly.*)
Your majesty—
(*Cornwallis hesitates and then takes a step forward and speaks measuredly.*)

CORNWALLIS

Your majesty, a nation's greatness depends upon its soldiers—

PITT

(*Throwing out his hands disgustedly as he sags down on his crutches.*)
Hah!

CORNWALLIS

(*Going on unperturbed.*)
When wars are fought soldiers are killed. England needs her soldiers. Let us not lose them.

KING GEORGE

(*A little querulously.*)
—Yes.

CORNWALLIS

If his majesty would send forth his stern but just proclamation to these rebels—declaring his wish for peace and amity—still—

VOICES

No! No!

OTHER VOICES

Impossible!

KING GEORGE

(*Curtly.*)
Your counsel, my lord?

Cornwallis

That the lives of countless young men—the flower of England—be spared—
(In a gesture of obedient salute.)
—spared to defend us against our more ancient enemies who still wait an auspicious time to fall upon us again.
(His eye sweeps by the two ambassadors.)

King George

You advise that I, King of England, bend the knee to those who have sinned against my person and against Almighty God whose chosen vassal I am.

Cornwallis

(Bowing.)
Your majesty.

King George

How better could the lives of our soldiers be spent than in upholding the honor of the crown.
(Cornwallis shows in his attitude he has no more to say. He steps back to his place.)

Pitt

(Pushing his point as the scene is silent.)
If this fleet sails against America, not only will Virginia rise, but the colonies will break from the authority of the crown and declare themselves free and their own masters.

King George

(Looking up as he indicates the document in his hand.)

My lord is reduced again to quoting this rebel Jefferson.
  (*Sardonically.*)
In the infirmity of thy mind thou hast lost the courage that once made thy name a fear and scourge to England's foes.

Pitt

(*His voice springing loudly in the air.*)
And when they have broken from us, mark my word, they will not fight unaided.
  (*He nods coldly and definitely toward the two ambassadors who move uneasily in their tracks.*)
Not only will we be forced to wage war across three thousand miles of treacherous ocean, but we will be set upon from Europe, and we will have to fight for our life —against France, against Spain.

Two Ambassadors

(*Quickly, almost in unison.*)
Your majesty, we protest! We—

Pitt

(*Almost weepingly.*)
I plead not the cause of the rebels, but that of my country, your country and mine—England. Shall she live or shall she die!
  (*He gazes with old and sick eyes before him. The king seems to be pondering.*)

King George

(*Finally in a quiet voice.*)
In all things we do not act over-hasty.
  (*A thought hitting him, and then the decision.*)

THE COMMON GLORY 39

The words of our General Cornwallis will be taken into advisement.

PITT

(*With a broken cry.*)
Thank God!

KING GEORGE

(*Sternly to Pitt, now the German steel in his voice.*) And as for you, my lord, you are now dismissed my presence to await my judgment upon you!
(*To North.*)
Tomorrow we will call the council concerning these matters.

PITT

It counts not what happens to me so England be saved.
(*He turns and starts moving slowly and painfully away. It is as if all the fire and strength have gone out of him now and his will is scarcely sufficient to drag his weary flesh and bones along. A messenger comes hurrying in by him and toward the throne. Pitt stops and slowly turns to look after him as he goes up and hands a paper to Lord North and then retires backward toward the right rear. North looks at the paper and is shocked.*)

KING GEORGE

(*Staring at him.*)
Yes?

LORD NORTH

(*Apologetically.*)
Later, your majesty.
(*Calling to the Major-domo.*)
Music!

(*The obedient organ makes a swirl of sound, not waiting for the musicians.*)

Major-domo
The dance! Music!

King George
(*Irritably and loudly to North.*)
The message!
> Lord North hesitates, then bows and hands him the paper. The organ is silent. He takes it from him and looks at it. For a moment he is dumfounded. He sinks slowly down into his chair.)

Ah—
> (*The courtiers and guests look at him in concern. His face grows heavy and dull. Finally he lifts his head.*)

My Lord Cornwallis, thou dost advise us far too late.
> (*A low grim chuckle begins to sound from him.*)

It seems we all do stand—hah—in grievous error.
> (*Almost as if enjoying the suffering in his heart.*)

My beloved people, a bloody battle has taken place again in New England—at—at—Bunker Hill. Hundreds of our soldiers lie wounded and dead.
> (*Exclamations of sorrow and anger break from the group. The king raises his hand for silence.*)

Hearken ye! Afflictions tread one upon the other. Virginia has risen to arms against us—the city of Williamsburg is in the hands of the rebels—
> (*Loudly.*)

—and the rightful and royal governor of that province, the Earl of Dunmore, has been forced to flee.
> (*The scene grows suddenly still.*)

Gordon

(*With a groan.*)
Impossible! No, your majesty. No.
(*Eileen looks up at her father and clings suddenly to his arm.*)

Voices

(*In ghastly whispers.*)
No! No!
(*Old Pitt's form seems to sag down even lower on his crutches. King George springs to his feet. He tears the message and the document of Jefferson into shreds and casts them from him. His face is almost convulsed with anger, and his words rise in a running soliloquy of passionate hate. The little dwarf peers quizzically up at him through his sightless mask.*)

King George

Ten thousand soldiers, twenty thousand soldiers, a hundred thousand soldiers—a hundred ships, a thousand ships! I will ransack all Europe, call upon all my kinsmen, draw in the English power from the uttermost parts of the earth and take my vengeance on these who have dared to raise their impious hands against me.
(*Lifting his eyes in burning intensity and as if speaking directly to some power in the air.*)
Hear me, our Father! Nor day nor night will I cease till this rebellion be put down—until I have taken the heads of these traitorous leaders and emptied them of their poisonous blood—yea drop by drop on London Bridge—in payment for their crimes!
(*As if beside himself, he suddenly rushes down from the dais toward Lord Pitt.*)

And thou bringer of evil—out of my sight—out!
(*He tries to strike the aged minister. Cornwallis and North restrain him.*)

North and Cornwallis

Your majesty.

Pitt

(*Drawing himself up.*)
So in this mad fellow here—
(*He hits the floor with his crutch.*)
—mark him—the degradation of our race.
(*Loudly.*)
And as England falls so shall America rise! For now the true Englishmen live beyond the sea.
(*With a cry.*)
Long live America!
(*He hobbles away swiftly into the darkness at the left front. The hisses of the courtiers follow after him. North helps the half-weeping king back to the throne. Gordon watches the king, then suddenly takes Eileen's arm.*)

Gordon

We must leave, my child—now—
(*To Cornwallis.*)
We speed our return to Virginia immediately—tonight—
(*With a grim smile as Cornwallis gazes at him.*)
—to prepare for your coming, my lord.
(*He extends his hand.*)

Cornwallis

(*Taking it.*)
Then it shall be soon.

(*Gordon looks about him at the scene, glances toward the distrait monarch again and then starts moving toward the right front. Cornwallis moves with him and Eileen.*)
And the preparation will be—er—thorough, I know.

Gordon

If it costs my life's blood it shall.
(*Eileen looks up at her father, holding tight to his arm.*)

Cornwallis

And the ships and arms and men I bring shall be sufficient.

Gordon

Good, good.
(*Stiffly.*)
His majesty is ill. Convey my regrets.
(*Cornwallis bows. The king is seen pushing North's helpful hand away, for now he is near the throne and feels its calming influence. He stretches out his arms to heaven, lifting his face in prayer.*)

King George

Almighty and everlasting God.
(*His voice soars up unashamedly and with fierce and piteous pleading in the air.*)
Hear thou the prayer of this thy servant in this hour! Let thy wrath and thy vengeance be certain and swift upon the enemies that now have risen in the earth against me.
(*Many of the people begin to get down on their knees.*)

44   THE COMMON GLORY

People

Hear our prayer, O God!
>(*Others begin to get down. Gordon, Eileen and Cornwallis stop at the right front in a momentary attitude of deference. The flag-bearer dips the flag in respect. The little dwarf sinks to his knees also, still peering up at the king. North and the ambassadors remain standing but with bowed heads.*)

King George

(*Loudly, wildly.*)
And thou hearest me! Now thou answerest me!
>(*With an exultant cry, his hands becoming two clenched fists reached above him.*)

In thy name we shall conquer!—Victory! Victory! To arms!
>(*The organ crashes into the loud first phrase of "Rule Britannia" and holds it in a sustained and surging dissonance.*)

(*The scene blacks out, and the light comes up on the narrator.*)

Narrator

(*Above his book as before.*)
The perverse and blinded king let loose his power against the rebellious colonies, and as Pitt had prophesied this but strengthened their determination to resist—even to

death. And in the south and in the north, the leaders fired the people to the cause of liberty and incited them to arms. George Washington was appointed commander-in-chief of the American forces. The Continental Congress was called at Philadelphia in May, 1776, to devise means for prosecuting the war, and here in Williamsburg in that same month a group of great Virginians, led by the matchless George Mason, issued forth one of the immortal documents of all time in man's long march—yours and mine—toward freedom—the Virginia Declaration of Rights. Here likewise these same men, inspired by the fervent Richard Henry Lee, brought forward another document—their resolution for independence—the first to do so in the new world. It was a fateful step to take and was bitterly debated before it came to a vote.

(The light fades from the narrator and comes up on the right side stage.)

SCENE 3

The hall of the house of burgesses, Williamsburg, Virginia. It is a place of sturdy but tasteful paneling and furniture. At the center rear is the presiding officer's tall-topped chair, and winging out on either side the curved long seats for house and committee members. In the shadow at the rear and on the sides are a large number of representatives, some standing, some sitting—among them Richard Bland, Paul Carrington, Archibald Cary, Bartholomew Dandridge, Dudley Digges, Benjamin Harrison, Patrick Henry, Thomas Jefferson, Richard Henry Lee, Thomas Ludwell Lee, James Madison, George Mason, Thomas Nelson, Robert Carter Nicholas, Mann Page, Edmund Randolph, Champion Travis, George Wythe and others. The forceful and scholarly Edmund Pendleton is in the president's chair. Robert Gordon is standing in the center of the scene, his figure highlighted, emphasizing his robust personality and strong face and rich dress. He is speaking with almost juridical weight and gravity, and with restrained but passionate feeling.

GORDON

(*Continuing.*)
—We have had inconveniences, true. The Stamp Act we protested. It was rescinded. The Navigation Act has been oppressive. Agreed. The Boston Port Bill has been unwise. English soldiers have invaded our soil. True. We acknowledge it. The blood of fighting men, English and

American, has been shed upon the battlefield. These evils have happened.

(*Sternly*.)

But they are small indeed compared to those that will follow if you allow yourselves to be deluded into taking this mad step of independence.

VOICES

We are not afraid. We'll take it.

(*Gordon holds up his hand. Such is his dignity and position among his fellows that they are silent in respect to him.*)

GORDON

The king alone is not England. England is old and glorious and has existed long before parliaments and kings, has endured many tyrannous and evil-minded servants and rulers and shall endure more. Still her glory, her greatness, her ideals of liberty, of justice shall continue.

(*Vehemently*.)

We must again plead our cause with the king and parliament.

VOICES

(*A little jeeringly*.)

Petition, petition!

GORDON

Gentlemen, liberalism and just authority will yet come back to England. And men like the great Pitt and Edmund Burke and Charles Fox and Rockingham will again be heard and heeded in the house of parliament. Your wrongs will then be righted.

Voices

And how long will that be? Too late! Too late!

Another Voice

They are your wrongs too.

Gordon

(*Loudly.*)
I solemnly warn you—if you persist in this intent of independence you will be destroyed.
 (*Holding up his hand.*)
Do France and Spain love England? They do not. Do they love us? They do not. Weakened and cut off from our mother country, we will fall a prey to their ravaging hand. France will take all of Canada back, take back the wide stretches of the northwest country. We will not be able to defend them. The Spanish will move boldly up the Mississippi and shut us in from the south and west. It is madness to think we—thirteen weak colonies of three million people—nearly a third of them black slaves—can stand against the mighty power of England, of France and Spain combined.
 (*Fiercely, loudly.*)
Gentlemen, I denounce this impious and insane resolution! It must be tabled. And I call upon this assembly now to adjourn!
 (*He turns and sits down. A round of applause comes out of the shadows for him.*)

Voices

Adjourn! Adjourn!

Other Voices

No! No!

STILL OTHER VOICES

Vote! Vote! Let us vote.
(*The light dims out on the scene at the right and comes up quickly on the narrator.*)

NARRATOR

And there were others who spoke against the measure, grave and judicious and learned men who like Robert Gordon feared the consequences of so bold a step. There were champions for it—the man who initiated the matter himself, Richard Henry Lee, the learned Richard Bland, the suave and cautious Edmund Pendleton, the mighty George Mason, the young and stubborn Thomas Jefferson.

(*The light fades from the narrator and comes up again quickly on the hall of the burgesses. Thomas Jefferson is speaking. He is a tall rawbony gangling youngish man of some thirty-two or three. His angular face is lighted by two intent clear blue eyes and is in its way rather handsome. His hair is sandy, inclining to a reddish color, his jaw strong, his nose prominent and slightly up-turned. He gives one the impression of possessing a sort of fibered character, of strength and tough endurance—a man already of immense concentrated power and patience and unyielding determination. His way of speaking is of the simplest, but his very sincerity demands and gets the closest attention from his hearers. His dress is simple but in fine taste.*)

JEFFERSON

(*Continuing.*)
One by one we have seen our rights and liberties perishing from us. It is argued that Mother England is sound

at heart and that only the parliament and mayhap the king are corrupted and therefore we must retain our loyalty and our connection with England.
(*He looks over at Gordon.*)
Who is England? England today consists of six million misguided, ignorant and enslaved people—

Voices
Hear! Hear!

Jefferson
(*Continuing.*)
—held under the power of one hundred and sixty-five thousand men who have the right of suffrage—and they alone—and can vote whatever laws they selfishly desire. A hundred and sixty-five thousand prejudiced voices declaring the laws of England, sending their representatives to parliament, not only determining the laws of that country but laws for us—nearly four million men—men who have won our self-reliance and our strength—from the long unending struggle with the wilderness—three thousand miles away from England. The rights and principles of government and humanity which we have derived and built here from this struggle are being destroyed in a corrupted motherland. Shall we cut ourselves loose from this corruption and keep clean these ideals and the heritage which we came to this new world to find or shall we be corrupted with her!

Voices
No! No!

Jefferson
Shall we yield up our integrity as men and accept the dictates of a hundred and sixty-five thousand Tory

voters, ruled over by a depraved parliament and a half-mad tyrant king? Shall we!

Voices

(*Accompanied by loud applause.*)
Never! Never!

Jefferson

(*Continuing, his voice deepening.*)
The hour of decision has come.... Gentlemen, as George Mason has said in this very chamber—for the first time in the history of this world we have a privilege never given to civilized man before—the privilege of beginning anew, here, now, a government of free men. This is a glorious challenge. It is an awful challenge. Nothing can be greater and nothing can be more worth the while. In the words of the immortal Patrick Henry, liberty or death. But let it not be death! Let it be liberty and life, life for the ideal we serve. Let us in prayer and dedication of spirit resolve now to take this step, to break free from a cruel and degenerate and blinded motherland and lift our faces toward the light, a new people, and under God and under heaven dedicate ourselves to establishing here on this earth a government of righteousness, of true liberty and of justice among men.
(*There is loud applause. The light blacks out from the side stage and comes up swiftly on the narrator.*)

Narrator

The resolution came to a vote and was over-whelmingly carried. Virginia had declared herself free from Britain. The call was sent out for troops to begin gathering here at Williamsburg, and Patrick Henry himself was appointed colonel commanding. Among the young men who flocked in to serve under him was Hugh Taylor, once a poor laboring lad here in Williamsburg but now a young pioneer in the western hills and friend of Jefferson. Down he came from the Albermarle, his head full of dreams and his heart still remembering the beautiful and proud Eileen Gordon of days gone by. Illuminations were held in the town, and the taverns and gaming tables were filled. But that great loyalist leader, Robert Gordon, and his followers took no part in these festivities. Nor did another well-known Williamsburger—our old friend Cephus Sicklemore, man of many words and no property, and public problem number one. A recent misdemeanor connected with Mis' Betty Randolph's chickens had somewhat restricted this latter gentleman's liberty and placed him in a position of discomfort down at the gaol house.

(*The light fades from the narrator and comes up on the left front of the center stage.*)

SCENE 4

In front of the gaol in Williamsburg. A scraggly mulberry tree shades over the scene. Here sitting on a drum of wood and tied by one leg to the stocks is Cephus Sicklemore. He is a huge lout of a man of middle-age, with hulking square shoulders, a big pot-belly and long legs. His jowled and unshaven face, especially as to his nose, is marked with the fires of gluttony and drink. He is dressed in nondescript clothes, an old weather-beaten three-cornered dark hat, a homespun shirt, a big and capacious-pocketed old coat, dirty buff trousers, baggy ragged stockings, and huge slipshod shoes. Up above him stuck to a post is a broad sign in a loud announcement—"Chicken Thief."

Sitting on a step over at the left and working at an open hymnbook is Peter Pelham, a quiet gray-haired man with sober dress. A big turkey-wing fan is going rhythmically in his hand. He is the Bruton Church organist and town gaoler. A big iron key ring and huge key lie on the step beside him. The muffled and drowsy singing of Negro dialect voices comes out of the prison in a rich harmony behind him. Cephus blinks about him and stirs restlessly. He opens his mouth in a great yawning gape of sleepiness and boredom.

Cephus

(*In a deep bass voice.*)
Ah-oohm.
  (*He scratches himself and for a moment sits with*

his chin propped dolefully in his hand. *The singing from the jail comes in on the scene.*)

PELHAM

(*Beating time in the air with his fan and humming above his hymnbook.*)
Ta-ta-de-da-de-da-ta-ta.
(*He turns over another page. Cephus smacks his lips and pulls out a huge handkerchief from one of his capacious pockets, a handkerchief half as large as a citizen's tablecloth. He gives his flaming nose a violent blowing, then replaces the cloth in his pocket.*)

CEPHUS

(*In his great bass voice.*)
There's a monstrous piece of hypocrisy loose in the world, Master Peter Pelham.
(*Pelham makes no reply.*)
This talk of liberty. Dang my heart! Where is it?
(*He jerks at his gyve, then gapes again. The singing comes in louder. He gestures toward the rear.*)
Them poor runaway slaves in there must be sweating buckets of sweat—in that gaol. I wager gold on it.

PELHAM

(*Abstractedly.*)
Gold, Cephus?

CEPHUS

Hah, hah, hah. Just a manner of speaking. Once I spent a night in that there place in February. Bejick and bejack, thought to my naked soul I'd burn up. Ahm—and speaking of the fiery furnace and the Hebrew children, as the Good Book says, I got religion that night.

Pelham

Would that it had lasted, Cephus.

Cephus

—Listen at 'em—pore souls.
   (*He joins in with the singing, humming along with his great voice lifted to falsetto.*)

'Way up on the mountain, heard my Savior say.

Pelham

You've got a good singing voice, Cephus. We need your held up in Bruton Church. Miserable sinner ye be—never once have you put foot in the door.

Cephus

Ah, you're wrong there, Master Pelham. Once I did and I made money at it, too.

Pelham

Money?

Cephus

That time the great Governor Dunmore christened his daughter Virginia. I was there. In the entrance I was, and when his honor come by I cried out, "Long live your worship!" Aye, that I did! And the great gentleman with all his lords and ladies shining in scarlet and gold and white lace and the flag above him, he says, "Give the good man a piece of gold." Hah-ha-hah! "Good man," he says. And he did so. Captain Foy it was give it to me—a new shining piece.

(He holds out his palm toward Pelham, then pulls it back and stares at it.)

PELHAM

And straight you went to the back door of the Raleigh Tavern and et yourself slap down under the table.

CEPHUS

(Gleefully.)
Aye, and next morning I woke up sick under Master Tazewell's apple tree. And the mocking-birds were singing like mad above me.
(His face swept with sudden piety.)
Aye, Master Pelham, I'm a poor sample of humanity.

PELHAM

Ye are indeed, Cephus. There ye be, tied again to the stocks, a public shame and disgrace—people passing along the street here to look at ye. And that good widow lady, Mammy Huzzitt, honing after ye. When will ye learn to mend your ways?

CEPHUS

(Cutting his eye around in dolorous sanctimony.)
The flesh is weak, Master Pelham.
(He pulls out his handkerchief again and wipes his eyes as if damming back a ready gush of tears.)
Still I wrastle like tarnation with that old Beelzebub. Ahm—ahm—yet he slips about me, layways me and ballyhacks me fore and aft. And in a weak moment down I come like a pitiful falling tree that the axes have hacked at. But there is a new day of freedom ahead they say and maybe grace will save me!

THE COMMON GLORY

(*He blows his nose again in a sonorous trumpet note.*)

Pelham

That's the first time I've ever heard a chicken called by the name of Beelzebub.

Cephus

Aye, Beelzebub in disguise. He kept crowing in my face and waking me.

Pelham

Sleeping in Miss Betty's hen-house, Cephus?

Cephus

Nay, down by the plum thicket. He was roosting there. (*Pelham chuckles.*)

Pelham

Ta-te-ta-ta.

Cephus

(*After a moment.*)
Is it music ye be choosing for the church o' Sunday, sir?

Pelham

It is. And a mortal fine hymn I've found.

Cephus

Aye, many's the time I pass the old church and hear the songs of praise sounding within—Master George Wythe in his high tenor and Master Edmund Pendleton and Master Richard Bland and Master Archibald Cary and Master Peyton Randolph and big Benjy Harrison—all

singing away. Beautiful. I used to hear young Thomas
Jefferson singing there too, him that played the fiddle
with Governor Fauquier in the palace and that's causing
most of the trouble now, they say. Yea, and gentleman
George Washington—long 'fore he was thoughted to
be a great general—we come there to Bruton Church to
pray and be blest, him and me—that time we marched
away with Braddock's army.

Pelham

(*Scoffingly.*)
Braddock's army, Cephus? Go 'long.

Cephus

That I was a soldier in it!—fighting the French and Indians out in the wilderness long 'fore ye come here to
play the organ in Williamsburg. Whiff! Whiff! The
bullets flying. And the poor lads dropping all around
me in a fervor of hot death. Massacre, mommick, and
murder 'twas. And crunch, crunch—like ripe grapes after
a big wind in the woods that day—was the eyeballs scattered on the ground. Heh, heh, heh!

(*Pelham throws up his hand in disgust. Entering
along the right front comes Mammy Huzzitt. She is
a plumpish, stout little widow-woman, energetic
and fiery, and dressed in good homemade dress and
apron, brogan shoes and a bonnet hanging back of
her neck. Her brownish hair, slightly speckled with
gray, is combed primly back. She carries a basket
on her arm. Cephus rises quickly to his feet.*)

Cephus

(*Pulling off his hat in a wide bow.*)
Mammy Huzzitt! Lady of my life—my joy—ah, the
moon and the stars they shine again!

Mammy Huzzitt

Don't lady of joy me, you old—chicken thief!

Cephus

Tarry, tarry, sight of my eyes.
(*Mammy Huzzitt moves along and then stops and stares at him as his words begin to flow.*)
Here on the soft bosom of this sacred earth I lift up my hands and swear for your sake, your sweet mercy-giving, your healing presence, I repent, I repent.
(*He falls on his knees.*)

Mammy Huzzitt

(*Scornful.*)
Liar, liar, you mad liar!

Cephus

Lord ha' mercy. Like music, like water to a perished man—the sound of your voice. Sweet lady, angel lady.

Mammy Huzzitt

You deceiver, you devil! Ah, the fine gush of words to destroy a woman's soul.

Cephus

(*Happily.*)
Wonderful!

Mammy Huzzitt

(*Taking an angry step back toward him.*)
Night and day, aye, me a poor widow woman, weaving and spinning and cooking to feed my orphan children. And you—a thousand times you swore to take me to

the altar and become a father unto them. And at my table I feed you and what do you do? You go stealing chickens.
(*Lamentingly.*)
And you never bring me any!

Cephus

Ah Lord, my lovely!
(*He holds out his arms to her.*)

Pelham

(*Chuckling ironically above his book.*)
Ha-ha.

Mammy Huzzitt

(*Angrily.*)
Whist on your tongue, Master Pelham.

Cephus

(*Bowing up and down.*)
Noble woman, soft-feeling woman—but most virtuous—
(*Casting up his eyes.*)
And fruitful!—My darling!

Mammy Huzzitt

(*Trying to resist him and then failing as is her weakness with him.*)
Oh, Cephus.
(*He seizes her hand and kisses it, then peeps into her basket.*)

Cephus

Are ye off to the market?

Mammy Huzzitt

Aye—just there—and to fetch my orphans to see the flags flying and the soldiers parading up and down.
(*She gestures.*)

Cephus

(*Eagerly.*)
And the pastries. You won't forget the pastries, my lamb.
(*He lifts up his hand in an oath.*)
This time I take the oath.

Mammy Huzzitt

There's not enough pastries in all Williamsburg for that bottomless belly of yours.
(*Giving his string belt a playful yet fierce jerk.*)
But I won't forget.

Cephus

(*Stretching out his great hands.*)
My bird. Hie thee fast. Hunger doth ravage my innards to distraction—a mighty rumbling doth afflict me from stem to stern.

Mammy Huzzitt

Yes, yes.
(*She takes a few tripping steps toward him, then stops.*)
You swear!

Cephus

(*Closing his eyes and holding up both his hands—fervently.*)
I do. I will marry ye!
(*While his eyes are closed she darts up to him, gives him a swift little pecking kiss on his rough glutton-burnt face and darts away. Cephus, in a transport*

and forgetting himself, plunges spontaneously after
her and falls headlong to the ground, tripped by the
gyve fastened to his ankle. Peter Pelham looks over
at him and breaks into a laugh, seeing him there
a moment resting on his hands and knees, his head
hanging down. Cephus vents his spleen into the air
with a loud snort.)

Bah!

(*He climbs slowly and dolefully up and resumes his
seat. Thomas Jefferson and Patrick Henry come
along from the left. With them is Hugh Taylor, a
young frontiersman of some twenty-five or six.
Jefferson is dressed in the plain but fine clothes of
a Virginia squire—hat, cape, knee breeches and
shiny-buckled shoes. He carries a sort of briefcase
stuffed with legal papers under his arm. Patrick
Henry is splendidly dressed in a new-fitted uniform
designating him as a colonel of the First Virginia
Regiment. He carries a sword in his hand with
which he now and then cuts at the grass. He is a
man about forty years old, rather tall, and with lean
hawk-like face and deep-set blue eyes. Hugh Taylor
is dressed in stout outdoor clothes, topped off by a
coonskin cap, and carries a long rifle held loosely
in the crook of his arm, also a blanket roll slung
over his shoulder, powder horn and cartridge pouch
at his belt. He is a handsome young fellow about
Jefferson's height, well-knit, lithe and with swift-
glancing somewhat humorous dark eyes and a firm
strong face. His motions and speech are quick, energetic and even restless, suggesting a turmoil and tear
of youth and life at work within him. He is representative of that type of American bred in the spa-
cious and sinewy outdoor life of the new world
—determined, forward looking, self-reliant—in fact,*

much like *Jefferson and Henry themselves. Cephus rises and pulls off his hat obsequiously.*)

JEFFERSON

(*As they come along*)
If there is one man to keep the colonies united in this war, it is General George Washington.

HENRY

I concur. The news from the north is good. New England and New York are rallying behind him.

JEFFERSON

And Virginia must furnish him with men and arms to the limit.
(*Almost passionately.*)
She will, she will!

HUGH

I will gladly raise a company myself in Albemarle.

JEFFERSON

Good, Hugh Taylor, good.

HENRY

Aye.

CEPHUS

(*Calling out.*)
Long live your honors.

HENRY

Well, Cephus Sicklemore.
(*Mr. Pelham rises.*)

PELHAM
(In greeting.)
Gentlemen.
JEFFERSON AND HENRY
(Nodding.)
Mr. Pelham.
CEPHUS.
(Staring at Henry admiringly.)
Aih, Lord, Patrick Henry, sir, that new uniform do become you. Like something sprung out of a band-box ye be. Nobody would know it was the same Patrick Henry that used to be—hmn—
HENRY
(With a laugh.)
—so be-draggled and be-drug?
CEPHUS
But your tongue made up for it, sir. I mind me of the day I stood in the door of the capitol there—
(He gestures off to the left.)
—and I heard you say—"Give me liberty or give me death!"
HENRY
That was in the church at Richmond, Cephus.
(Feeling the blade of his sword.)
I was ready to fight that day and I'm ready to fight now.
(He cuts the air a swishing blow. Cephus springs out of the way with a squeak.)
CEPHUS
Aye, sir, aye. And please your honor, whilst ye're a-cutting with that there sword—will you whack this here chain in two—

(*He holds up a manacled foot.*)
—with which they've bound down a poor innocent son of liberty.

JEFFERSON

Law and order, Cephus, law and order.
(*He turns toward Pelham.*)

CEPHUS

(*Piteously.*)
Please, sir, Mr. Jefferson.
(*Jefferson gestures dismissingly toward Cephus.*)

JEFFERSON

(*To Pelham.*)
The Tory list—is it ready? Our Committee has need of it this evening.

PELHAM

(*Touching his forefinger to his hat.*)
All ready, sir. I'll fetch it.
(*He goes off into the shadow at the left.*)

HUGH

(*Laughing.*)
You'd been stealing the last time I saw you here, Cephus. Five years a-gone, it was.

CEPHUS

(*Peering at him, his face breaking into a great smile.*)
Odds flinders and balls, if it ain't Hugh Taylor!

HUGH

It is, old lad.

CEPHUS

And back in Williamsburg. Thought ye'd wiped the dust of this Sodom place forever from your feet.

HUGH

I've come down from the hills to join Colonel Henry's regiment.

CEPHUS

(*Distastefully.*)
Ahm—war.

HUGH

(*Heartily.*)
True. And me'n old long-barrel are in it to the end.
(*He slaps his rifle barrel and swings it by Cephus who backs out of the way.*)

CEPHUS

(*Grimacing.*)
Fee-foe-fum. Uhm—and just yistiddy ye were a young gosling boy, fetching and carrying here in Williamsburg all harmlesslike.

HUGH

(*A little harshly.*)
Aye, fetching and carrying, true enough.

CEPHUS

(*Winking.*)
But all was not slavery—eh? Your eyes were mighty loose, eh, lad?—making free and worshipful with a certain trick of satin and velvet—little Mistress Eileen Gordon.

HUGH

(*Roughly, almost bitterly.*)
A double-tongued liar and a thief!

Cephus

(*Smacking his lips.*)
And now—and Colonel Henry and Mr. Jefferson will bear me out—she's purtier'n ever—purtier'n any red apple hanging high—
(*He emphasizes the word "high."*)
—in Master George Wythe's garden.

Jefferson

Cephus has a keen eye for beauty. I trust it will be as sharp in aiming a gun against our enemies.
(*Cephus throws up his hands.*)

Cephus

War, war, the world's gone mad. Deliver me!

Henry

The Committee is issuing a call, Cephus. And Sergeant Jack is instructed to go about the town crying it.

Cephus

Lord, your reverence, I don't even know how to shoot a musket.
(*Pelham comes in from the shadows at the left rear in time to hear the erstwhile old braggart's words. He clears his throat sardonically. Cephus quickly resumes his seat on the stocks.*)

Pelham

(*Handing Jefferson the foolscap paper.*)
A number of our rich planters along the James are in that list, sir.

Henry

(Cutting at the grass again with his sword, his voice suddenly hard.)

They shall be taken care of.

Jefferson

They shall.

(The three men nod to Pelham and start on out. Pelham returns to his book. Cephus rises and steps out in front of Jefferson, grabbing his arm and calling pleadingly up to him.)

Cephus

Please sir, your honor, tyranny and oppression it is. 'Tis notorious-like how you love the common man. Well, sir, I'm a poor common man—a most common man, your worship! Help me.

Jefferson

(Kindly but firmly.)

And a common man should learn to behave himself, Cephus.

(The three men move on. A bevy of young women come along the street from the right. There are some six or eight of them all dressed in bright summer garments, kerchiefs and cute little be-ribboned bonnets and a few of them carrying pink and blue parasols to shade themselves from the sun. Among them are Eileen Gordon and Sarah Hallam, the pretty Williamsburg dancing teacher. Cephus turns forlornly and disgustedly back to his seat. Hugh gazes out at the young ladies as they enter chattering away.)

FIRST YOUNG LADY

Oh, the minuet, Miss Hallam!

SECOND YOUNG LADY

The galop, don't forget the galop!

MISS HALLAM

We'll dance them all.
(*Jefferson and Henry bow to the young ladies.*)

JEFFERSON

Cousin Eileen, Miss Hallam.

HENRY

Mistress Gordon, Mistress Hallam.
(*Miss Hallam curtseys slightly but Eileen does not.*)

EILEEN

(*Somewhat coldly.*)
Cousin Jefferson.
(*At the mention of Eileen's name Hugh has turned and fastened his dark eyes upon her. The girls start on by. Jefferson reaches out and touches Eileen's arm.*)

JEFFERSON

And Cousin Robert, he keeps well?

EILEEN

He does.
(*Her voice is still cold, her manner aloof.*)

JEFFERSON

Colonel Henry and I had hoped to pay our respects and hear the latest news from London.

EILEEN

Father receives few callers these days.

JEFFERSON

Indeed.
   (*Genially.*)
We'd heard differently. Eh, Colonel Henry?

HENRY

Differently, very differently.
   (*Eileen looks at the two men a little searchingly.*)

JEFFERSON

And your birthday ball is tonight?

EILEEN

It is.

MISS HALLAM

We're on our way to the Apollo Room now for our dancing lesson.

JEFFERSON

Never before, Cousin Eileen, have you failed to invite me—and my violin.

EILEEN

   (*Spiritedly.*)
I'm against all who are against his majesty, Cousin Jefferson.

Jefferson

And that's a great error, my child. And you mean against your father, don't you?
(*Suddenly taking her arm.*)
This gentleman you know—an old friend of ours.
(*Deliberately.*)
—Hugh Taylor.
(*Eileen starts ever the faintest bit, and she and Hugh stare at each other. Her hand goes out and takes Miss Hallam's arm.*)

Eileen

You've changed, Hugh Taylor.
(*Hugh slowly removes his coonskin cap.*)

Hugh

(*Gazing at her with spontaneous admiration.*)
For the better, I hope. And you—you are—
(*His words die out as he looks at her.*)

Eileen

Then I've changed too. Very well. For this is a time of change.
(*With sudden accusation as she looks at him.*)
And if with that rifle you have come down to fight against your king—

Hugh

I have.

Eileen

Then in mercy's name go back again, go back to those forsaken hills where you belong.
(*She gives the three men a sudden sunshiney smile,*

mixed with acid, and she and Miss Hallam hurry away. Hugh gazes after her. Cephus clears his throat loudly and sardonically.)

Cephus
Ahm!

Henry
Fire and brimstone—like her father.

Cephus
(Cackling and slapping himself.)
Sweet red apple high in a tree—and a cat may look at a king.

Hugh
Whist, ye blabber mouth!

Jefferson
(Taking Henry's arm a little confidentially as the three men start on.)
A birthday ball—rather clever of Cousin Robert—

Henry
Uhm—

Jefferson
We must look into the matter. Some of our liberty boys mayhap would have interest at this ball—

Henry
I concur. They would.
(He cuts the air viciously with his sword as they go out. Cephus watches them with rheumy and splenetic eye.)

Cephus

Monstrous hypocrisy, Master Pelham. Talk, talk.
(Indicating himself.)
And the poor do suffer in vain.
(Pelham hums unconcernedly above his book. Cephus' chin sinks sorrowfully down on his hands again. The clangor of a bell is heard approaching at the left, and the voice of the town crier.)

Town Crier

(Calling.)
Hear ye, hear ye!
(The bell comes nearer, the voice likewise.)
Proclamation! Proclamation!
(The town crier enters, accompanied by a stalwart young patriot soldier in uniform, Sergeant Jack. The crier stops and holds out a document in front of him, his voice soaring through the air.)
Let it be known that the Committee of Safety of the province of Virginia doth hereby call on all citizens one and sundry to repair to the palace green at the Duke of Gloucester Street to witness a show of arms.
(He gives the bell a ring.)
And likewise hear ye—hear ye!

Sergeant Jack

(Bawling out.)
And whosoever will enlist in the service of this colony shall be freed from his confinement or misdemeanors whatsoever.

Town Crier

Hear ye! Hear ye!

CEPHUS

Eigh! Hist!—Freed, ye say?
  (*He stands up.*)

SERGEANT JACK

Aye, freed.
  (*He comes over to Cephus.*)

CEPHUS

Hearken, Mr. Pelham, hearken to that!

PELHAM

  (*Looking up.*)
Aye, and what for a soldier would ye make?

CEPHUS

  (*Blankly.*)
Uhm—soldier.

SERGEANT JACK

  (*As before.*)
And bounty money—
  (*He emphasizes the word money.*)
—shall be paid on the signing.
  (*He jingles a purse at his waist.*)

CEPHUS

Money!—Ye hear that, Mr. Pelham.
  (*Eagerly.*)
Quick with your key. I'm a free man.

PELHAM

Ye'll never make a soldier, Cephus.
  (*The soldier begins to feel Cephus.*)

THE COMMON GLORY

Sergeant Jack

Sound in body and limb?

Cephus

(*Gleefully.*)
Twang, twang! Sound as Spanish gold. Unlock me, Master Pelham.
(*The soldier pinches him suddenly and Cephus lets out one of his soaring howls. Then Sergeant Jack examines him somewhat like a horsetrader.*)

Sergeant Jack

Uhm-uhm. I doubt not he's winded and bellowsed in the bargain and in truth moon-eyed. But such as he is we will take him.

Cephus

(*Angrily.*)
Once I wrastled the great Bull Peters down—him that could muscle out an anvil on one hand and a hogshead of tobacco on the other—there by the English Coffee House —I did—and vast was the congregation that cheered me name on high.
(*Sergeant Jack eyes him once more, then makes up his mind.*)

Sergeant Jack

(*Sticking forward a tablet book.*)
With this lead make your mark.
(*Cephus makes his mark.*)
And take the oath.

Cephus

Aye.

Sergeant Jack

(*In a run of words.*)
"I swear on the mercy seat of Almighty God that I will to the utmost of my power support, maintain and defend the said province of Virginia against the said King George the Third of Britain, his heirs and successors and his or their abettors, assistants and adherents, so help me God!"

Cephus

(*Casting his eyes piously upward and holding up his right hand and speaking in a small voice.*)
I swear!

Sergeant Jack

(*To Peter Pelham.*)
Unloose him, as the decree declares.
(*Sternly to Cephus.*)
And meet me in Waller's Grove by twelve of the clock.

Cephus

Aye, aye, at once—or sooner.
(*He reaches out his hand for the money. The sergeant gives him a coin and Cephus stares at it joyously. He kisses it and bites it. Pelham gestures a shrugging acquiescence, comes forward, and unlooses the gyve. And Cephus steps free. He cavorts around a bit, trying out his leg. The crier moves on out at the left, accompanied by Sergeant Jack.*)

Town Crier

(*Calling and ringing his bell as he goes.*)
Hear ye! Hear ye!
(*Suddenly Cephus sets off running up the steps along the proscenium wall. Pelham gazes after him,*

THE COMMON GLORY

somewhat indulgently, somewhat contemptuously, then returns to his seat.)

PELHAM

(Resuming his music.)
Ta-te-ta-ta.
(A moment passes, and Mammy Huzzitt comes in with her laden market basket. With her are her four little children—two boys, two girls. They are barefooted and poorly dressed, but are bright-faced and cheery.)

MAMMY HUZZITT

(Staring at the empty stocks aghast.)
Lord ha' mercy—he's broke loose!

PELHAM

(Abstractedly.)
No. He's signed for a soldier—and off to the tavern.

MAMMY HUZZITT

(Wrathful and undone.)
Children, we've lost him again.
(Half-weeping, she leads the crying children off the way they came.)
Bah—a soldier! Well, when King Jarge hears it, he will lay down his arms!

PELHAM

(Beating time in the air.)
Ta-te-ta-ta.
(The light dies away from the scene and comes up on the narrator.)

Narrator

And while the gluttonous Cephus visits the tavern to eat up his new-found substance, the liberty boys make plans to pay a visit to Robert Gordon's house. That night Eileen's garden fete and ball were under way, and the leading Tories of the Tidewater had gathered there to do her honor as well as secretly to discuss matters of their own particular interest.

(*The light fades out from the narrator and comes up on the center stage in a bright illumination.*)

SCENE 5

The garden of Robert Gordon's house in Williamsburg. It is evening time and the place is one of magic, beauty, music, moonlight, and the grace and dress of eighteenth century Virginia. The scene is lighted with Japanese lanterns and is alive with a gathering of young Virginia aristocrats. At the back is a terrace with a couple of broad steps leading up to it. A sort of widestretching pergola crosses the scene behind the terrace, ending off at the left in a little summerhouse. Here in the summerhouse is a small orchestra, consisting of a flute, viola, a couple of violins, harpsichord and recorder. They are providing music for the scene. A long table is set on the terrace and a number of guests are seated and standing around it, being waited on with refreshments and drinks by black servants in livery. High up above the scene and far away at the back is the illuminated tip of the cupola on the governor's palace, surmounted above now by the new Virginia flag waving in the night air like a thing of flame alive.

On the lawn in front of the terrace a stately but swift-moving dance is under way. Some ten or twelve couples in bright and sparkling dress are moving rhythmically and happily to the music. The line of dancers stretches from the front on back toward the terrace at the rear, the men squiring their partners and bowing as the musicians play away.

THE COMMON GLORY

The front of the scene is illuminated by a bright spot of light near the footlights, and the rear of the scene diminishes into shadow. As the couples dance, they move toward the front of the stage and into this highlighted spot. They speak and then pass on into the shadow at the rear.

First Young Lady

I do so like this dance—uhm—wonderful.

First Young Man

Eileen's birthdays are always wonderful.

First Young Lady

Yes.
 (Glancing off.)
What a handsome couple she and Francis Corbin make.

First Young Man

I doubt not next year this time the ball will be a wedding celebration.

First Young Lady

If only this wretched quarrel with his majesty—

First Young Man

Pooh, pooh. It will all be ended in a six months.
 (They pass on. They are followed into the highlighted spot by a stoutish middle-aged woman and a weakish and feminish man of thirty-five or forty.)

Woman

(Her great jowled head nodding to the surge of the violins.)

Remember how we used to dance down at Rosewell at Christmas?
(*Musingly*.)
Ah, Rosewell—adorable John Page.

MAN

(*Spitishly*.)
Adorable Mrs. Page.

WOMAN

Yes, yes. Remember the night Patty Skelton first met Thomas Jefferson there. Love—passionate love it was. He bewitched her with his violin.

MAN

(*Scornfully*.)
Hah. Thomas Jefferson. De mortibus nil nisi bonum.

WOMAN

(*Sharply*.)
De mortuis—your Latin is bad. Besides he's not dead.

MAN

Still infamous be his name.

WOMAN

Yes, they say he and a few others will have to be hanged.
(*With a great sigh exuding into the night.*)
Well, so be it and things will be as they were.
(*They move rhythmically on back toward the rear. Another couple comes into the light. The lady is short and dumpy and merry and with a high hair-do*

THE COMMON GLORY 83

and rich in jewels and dress. This is Maria Byrd, wife of Colonel William Byrd III. Her companion is a young man of twenty or twenty-one.)

MRS. BYRD

(*Her body undulating with music under her clothes.*)
If only life were made of music! Wonderful, wonderful. As soon as these politics get settled we'll have a great ball at Westover. You must come and bring all your friends from the College of William and Mary.

YOUNG MAN

I'm afraid I haven't many friends there now, Cousin Maria. It is become a nest of rebels.

MRS. BYRD

(*Clucking.*)
Tchk, tchk. These rash times.
(*Appealingly.*)
And you and Francis Corbin are going away.

YOUNG MAN

We join Governor Dunmore at Norfolk tomorrow. And soon we will be back to Westover for the ball. Soon.

MRS. BYRD

(*Fervently.*)
God grant it.

YOUNG MAN

Reinforcements are pouring in and now a man-of-war is lying off Yorktown. Others will appear in the river at any time. These harum-scarum rebels will be scattered like leaves in a storm.

Mrs. Byrd

Yes, yes, I'm sure. Ah—poor Governor Dunmore.
(They move rhythmically on and back toward the rear. Eileen and Francis Corbin come into the light. Corbin is an aristocratic young man of twenty-five or twenty-six in lace and velvet and silver buckles and is obviously smitten with Eileen.)

Francis

(Looking down at her admiringly.)
I wager you set his majesty's head spinning—there in London.

Eileen

(Lightly.)
And all evening you've tried to set mine spinning—with compliments.

Francis

And why not?
(Intensely.)
I love you.
(She bows her head slightly as he goes on.)
Tonight I go away to serve my king. I've asked your father for your hand.
(She looks inquiringly up at him.)
And he wishes it. Our two great families will then be united.

Eileen

(Smilingly.)
Our two great plantations likewise.

Francis

Please, please. If you were a beggar maid I would love you.

Eileen

(*A little warmly as she looks at him.*)
I believe you, Francis.
(*Looking about suddenly, as if bothered by his devotion.*)
Where are father and Colonel Corbin?

Francis

(*Putting a finger to his lips.*)
S-s-h.
(*With a backward flick of his head.*)
They're having a meeting within.

Eileen

This trouble will soon be over. It will, won't it, Francis?

Francis

Of course. Men like your father will never yield.

Eileen

But men like Cousin Jefferson and Patrick Henry and Mr. Randolph. They're all stubborn men, all stubborn likewise.

Francis

Don't worry your pretty head. Let us be happy—now—for this evening. Let us be happy.

(*They turn away into the shadow. The light fades out on the center scene and comes up on the left side stage, representing a room in the Gordon mansion. It is a charming place with furniture and paneling of pure early Georgian style. A large portrait of King George the Third hangs on the rear wall. Gathered in this room are a dozen or more elderly and middle-aged Virginia aristocrats and loyalists—among them Ambler, Bucktrout, Burwell, Carpenter, Corbin, Hill, Ross, Sprowle and Wormley. Also present and in ecclesiastical dress is Dr. John Camm, the still loyalist president of the College of William and Mary. An old gray-haired Negro servant in livery is moving about replenishing the wine. Gordon is standing in the center of the scene, his glass in his hand.*)

Gordon

(*Sternly.*)
Let us not delude ourselves, my friends. We are certain to have bloodshed here in Virginia. The damage in Norfolk and Portsmouth has been done by fire—true. But the slaughter at Great Bridge shows these rebels can use the rifle as well as the torch. And now that Jefferson and Henry and the Adamses and their committees have set the entire thirteen colonies ablaze with the spirit of revolt—we know there must be fighting, heavy fighting ahead.

(*The men around the room nod solemnly.*)
In the end we shall win. But we must be patient—we must not lose our senses. We must keep firm—and patient.

(*Colonel Corbin clears his throat angrily. He is a choleric stout man of early middle age.*)

COLONEL CORBIN

Ah, these rebels—traitors! Next week my wife and I return to Fairfield and there we will stay—
(*Looking about him.*)
—quietly.

GORDON

That is the word—quietly.

VOICES

Aye. Aye.

GORDON

I expect to return to my plantation also shortly—there to watch and wait—
(*Impressively.*)
—and to work.

COLONEL CORBIN

Remember, in the autumn you're all to come to my plantation for the hunting. Zounds, peace must be restored by hunting time!

GORDON

And so my friends we understand what we must do.

VOICES

We understand.

GORDON

And now the good news. It is certain that General Cornwallis will be sent south when he arrives.
(*The reaction on the part of the men shows that this is indeed good news. There are ejaculations of "good," "bravo," etc.*)
We will prepare for his coming. Gentlemen, the time

will soon arrive when this first flush of rebel fervor has burnt itself out. Then with the full power of England landed upon these shores—then my friends, my friends—
  (*He gestures into the air.*)
Until then we keep the peace, we keep the peace—

Dr. Camm

And when he gives the word, gentlemen—the loyal people of Virginia will rise at Robert Gordon's command.
  (*He reaches out and shakes Gordon's hand.*)

Voices

Bravo, bravo! Robert Gordon! Gordon!

Other Voices

Cornwallis! Cornwallis!

Gordon

Thank you, Dr. Camm.
  (*Gesturing again.*)
And now, gentlemen—
  (*He lifts his glass in the air. The others rise quickly and hold their glasses extended in front of them. They all turn and face the portrait. Gordon's voice comes out strong and commanding.*)
To his majesty the king—and England forever!
  (*They drink in a fervent hush. The scene fades out. Immediately the light comes up in a great blaze on the center stage, much brighter than before. The garden is now a-swirl with bounding vitality and liveliness. The music and dancing have changed to a swift-stepped courante in time to an early English folk tune.*)

THE COMMON GLORY

(*Under the pulse beat and spell of the music some of the guests on the terrace have begun dancing in improvisation. Gordon and the aristocratic planters come in from the right rear. They immediately take partners from the ladies gathered on the terrace and enter into the general fun. The music and dance increase in spirit and fervor until even the black servants become infected with the rhythm, moving across the scene at the rear and carrying their trays of food in a sort of half-dance step of their own. The scene is suddenly swept by a loud and cacophonous surge of sound in the organ, and the harmony of the dance breaks into a distorted and wild discord, likewise the little orchestra. As the snarling organ repeats its warning, the musicians stop playing, and the dance is stilled altogether. A raggle-taggle group of young Virginia patriots bound into the scene, yelling like demons and many of them dressed in the outlandish garb and war paint of In-*

90   THE COMMON GLORY

dians and carrying war clubs and tomahawks in
their hands. Others wear the blue uniforms of the
First Virginia Regiment, among them Hugh Taylor
who is the leader of the band. He carries a sword
and looks handsome enough as a young lieutenant.
Some five or six black-hooded figures come along
behind bearing a tall catafalque contraption covered
by a dark cloth. The ladies scream in fright, the
servants bolt away, and for a moment the place is
in pandemonium. The organ adds its voice to the
turmoil in its snarling commentary and interpretation.)

(*Hugh leads his yelling compatriots about the scene.*)

Liberty Boys

Down with the king! Down with the Tories!
  (*By this time nearly all of the guests are escaped from the garden. But Eileen, like her father, remains.*)

Gordon

(Thundering at Hugh.)
Take this rout of cut-throats and ruffians from my house!
(The young patriots give him a loud boo. Hugh steps in front of Eileen and bows mockingly to her.)

Hugh

Dear lady, please to tell your father—this is not a picnic.
(Almost sweetly).
And as for his friends—
(Gesturing with his sword.)
—they'll likely get their heads cracked if they interfere.

Liberty Boys

Down with Robert Gordon!
(Eileen looks at Hugh with hard bright eyes.)

Eileen

How dare you to come here like this—Hugh Taylor!

Hugh

(Coolly.)
I dare well enough.
(Gordon starts and stares at him.)

Gordon

Hugh Taylor!

Hugh

Aye.
(Bitterly.)
Whose family worked in bondage many a year here on your plantation.

GORDON

Still the proud lip, the disrespectful tongue.
   (*Angrily.*)
You were free workers.

HUGH

Free—free to pile up profits in your barns and warehouses for you—to be spent here on all the frippery and moonlight and perfume and fops and spineless weaklings. It was our sweat, our blood!

GORDON

Silence!

HUGH

Hah! He commands me as of old. Do this, do that. You hewer of wood and drawer of water. Hah!
   (*His dark eyes glowing.*)
But there in the hills to the west I found my freedom and I've come to fight for it.
   (*He gestures toward his men with his sword. One of them pulls at a string attached to the catafalque and down comes the black covering, revealing a gallows from which the effigy of a Virginia aristocrat in all his fine dress is hanging. A knife is plunged in the heart of the figure, and a great stain of blood effuses itself down its white satin-clad side. Across and above the figure is nailed the big caption "Death to Tories!"*)
And we know the meaning of this birthday ball, sir—to gather your Tory friends here, to plan and plot.
   (*Pointing toward the effigy.*)
Well—there is how it will end—the hangman's noose! We warn you.
   (*Along the terrace at the rear two or three young aristocrats led by Francis Corbin now re-enter with*

THE COMMON GLORY

drawn swords. Hugh and a number of his men whirl toward them. For a moment it looks as if blood will be shed. Gordon interposes himself between them.)

Gordon

Put up your swords, men!
  (He keeps Corbin and the others back. The liberty boys now ring themselves about the scene and burst into a loud song.)

Liberty Boys

(As they march.)

We'll smite the Tor-ies hip and thigh, And rip their guts right mer-ri-ly, And hang their hides up high to dry, Fight-ing for lib-er-tee, Oh, what a sight! 'Tis my de-light To spill their blood, A crim-son flood, Hark, hark, hark, there's thun-der, Of can-non and drums un-der, And bay'nets cut-ting a-sun-der. And Vir-gin-ia's sons shall yet be free!

(*They march on down into the garden at the right front, continuing their song as they go. Hugh stands guardingly behind them, his sword in his hand. Sergeant Jack stops at the right front exit and remains there watchfully with his bayoneted rifle.*)

Eileen
(*Furiously.*)
Have you no respect—no shame?

Hugh
(*Shaking his head.*)
No, not tonight.

Gordon
(*His voice shaking with passion.*)
I warn you, Hugh Taylor—this madness will be over like an early April rain and those who have taken up arms will suffer, I tell you.

Hugh
(*Defiantly.*)
Suffer? We have already suffered.

Gordon
And the king will make you suffer more. Your leaders will be hanged in nooses already made for them—Jefferson, Washington and Adams—and you poor deluded followers will die in irons like common criminals.

Hugh
You have had our warning. Make the most of it.
(*Almost jubilantly.*)

A war is coming and a new day with it—and I'm going to help it come.
　　(*To Eileen.*)
And it will sweep over you and your father and others like him.

Eileen

You do not frighten us.

Hugh

Then like your father you're mad—mad.
　　(*He gazes deeply at her.*)
So it all must be settled in blood, Mistress Gordon.

Gordon

　　(*Abruptly.*)
Come, daughter.
　　(*He turns toward the terrace.*)

Hugh

And you, my lovely lady—I—
　　(*He stares at her, his words dying out.*)

Eileen

　　(*Vehemently.*)
Speak, speak!

Hugh

And the old ways are ending now.
　　(*In a strained voice, almost softly.*)
I'll remember you this way, Eileen Gordon—standing here in the moonlight—beautiful in the moonlight—and lonely and waiting.

Francis Corbin

The insolence!
(Gordon lays a restraining hand on Corbin's arm. Hugh shakes his head, his words rising with almost savage exultation.)

Hugh

A man could do anything for you, could climb high. Aye, march to battle, die for you—a man that is a man.
(Eileen looks at him almost startled, her head lifted, her body taut. Hugh starts away, then turns swiftly back.)
And in the days ahead, you'll need me—I know you'll need me. And then I'll come to you—and help you—
(He reaches out, grabs her hand and kisses it, then flings it half-angrily and disdainfully away from him. He strides quickly off following his men. She stands there gazing after him. Francis Corbin comes down the terrace toward her. The light fades out from the scene and rises on the narrator.)

Narrator

The spirit of liberty continued to spread among the people. And the resolution for independence of the entire thirteen colonies was introduced in Continental Congress by Richard Henry Lee. Thomas Jefferson by virtue of the power of his pen was immediately placed on a committee consisting of the venerable Benjamin Franklin, John Adams, Roger Sherman, and Robert Livingston to draw up a declaration. And following the committee's urging, he undertook the task himself. There in his room in a bricklayer's house in Philadelphia he worked many a hot summer night, writing out word by word and phrase by phrase the credo of his faith—

the credo on which this our young nation was to launch its existence.

(The light fades from the narrator and comes up on the right front of the center stage.)

SCENE 6

A room in a boardinghouse in Philadelphia—a plain place. There are a writing table, a chair or two and a cupboard. The floor is somewhat littered with rolled-up discarded wads of foolscap. When the light comes up on the scene, we see Jefferson seated in a chair with a writing-desk box across his lap. He has some foolscap manuscript spread out on the desk and is making corrections in it with a goosequill pen. He shows the great strain of his hard work. His hair is rumpled, his face haggard, his coat off and sleeves rolled up. He gathers up the manuscript, jostles the pages together and reads—his words evoked in the voice of the narrator from the darkness in a huge half-whisper.

Narrator

(As if testing out the words for their sound, their sense, their rhythm, even as Jefferson does in his mind.)

When in the course of human events it becomes necessary for one people to dissolve the political bands which have connected them with another, and to assume among the powers of the earth the separate station—

(Jefferson dips his pen into his inkwell and makes a correction. The narrator waits and makes the correction with him.)

—the separate and equal—station to which the laws of nature and of nature's God entitle them, a decent respect to the opinions of mankind requires that they should declare the causes which have driven them—

THE COMMON GLORY

(*Jefferson corrects again, the narrator with him.*)
—which impel them to the separation—We hold these truths as obvious—
(*Jefferson corrects, the narrator likewise.*)
—to be self-evident—
(*Jefferson studies the manuscript. The light fades down on him a bit and comes up slightly on the immediate fore-stage as if on a street running in front of the little house. Off to the right, we hear the approaching song of a sort of male quartet. Entering the scene from the right front come the elderly Benjamin Franklin, John Adams, young Robert Livingston, Roger Sherman and the devout and fanatical Sam Adams. They are all simply and plainly dressed, though Franklin and Livingston affect a touch more of lace and polish of silver-buckled shoes. These gentlemen are feeling good after a fat evening of Philadelphia socializing and with the exception of Sam Adams are indulging themselves in a song. The elderly Franklin is in front stepping somewhat limpingly though sprightlily along on a gouty foot and beating time in the air with a sporty silver-headed cane.*)

GROUP

(*Singing.*)

And we'll spit in old King George's eyes, With a 'fa la la la la la la. Good health un-to his en-e-mies, With a fa la la la la

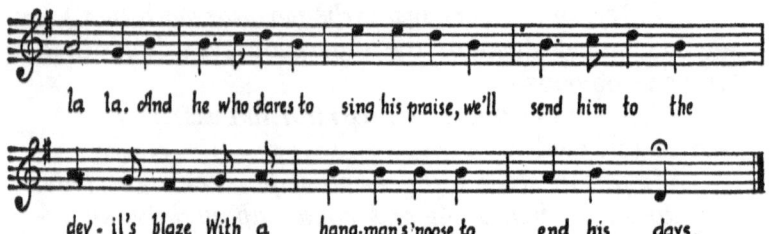

la la. And he who dares to sing his praise, we'll send him to the dev-il's blaze With a hang-man's 'noose to end his days.

(*They stop in a close group in front of the house to wind up with good barbershop harmony.*)

With a fa la la la la la la la la la la With a fa la la la la la la.

(*Franklin whams on the side of the house with his cane.*)

FRANKLIN

(*Loudly.*)
Jefferson!
    (*The light brightens on the interior of the room. Jefferson looks out.*)
Your committee again!
    (*The group of men, Franklin in front, tramp on into the room. Jefferson climbs to his feet to receive them.*)

JEFFERSON

Mr. Franklin—gentlemen.

FRANKLIN

(*Staring about.*)
Still hard at it, eh? We brought Sam Adams along—another partner in crime.

Jefferson

(*Bowing slightly.*)
I'm honored.

John Adams

(*A man of middle stature, bald-headed and quick of speech and gesture.*)
Shame—while we enjoy the fat of the land you labor here.

Franklin

Tut-tut, John Adams—and so it is with genius. Mediocre talents like ours always carry away the profit and the pleasure.

Sherman

(*As sincere as he is plainly dressed.*)
These Philadelphia social gatherings are no pleasure to me, I declare to you.

Jefferson

(*Wryly.*)
Nor any profit, I wager.

Franklin

You're wrong.
(*Jovially.*)
For we dine and feast—in spite of plaguey gout—for a purpose.

Livingston

(*Young and eager, a courteous gentleman.*)
True, for we must keep Madame Morris and her wealthy friends happy. We shall need money. She continues to inquire after you, Jefferson.

Jefferson

I've sent my apologies—pleading the press of business.
(*He indicates the manuscript.*)

Franklin

(*Picking up a little framed picture from the table—to Jefferson.*)
Your wife—Mistress Patty?

Jefferson

Yes.

Franklin

She must be a great comfort. She's beautiful.

Jefferson

She is!
(*Franklin passes the picture on to John Adams, who along with the others looks at it.*)

John Adams

I don't wonder you are eager to return to Monticello.

Jefferson

(*Staring off, his face caught in worry for an instant.*)
She's ill and needs me—and our baby...
(*His voice dies out.*)

Franklin

(*Striking the table with his cane.*)
This creating a new country is no bed of roses, gentlemen. It's a dog's life for all of us—moving, riding, work-

ing, never able to be at home, separated from our loved ones.

Sam Adams
But future generations will remember us.

Franklin
Dod drat it, I'm interested in this generation.

Sam Adams
It's a privilege to die for liberty.

Franklin
(*Impatiently.*)
And what liberty is there under six foot of earth? Go ahead and die, Sam Adams, I want to live, I'm seventy years old but I still want to live.

Voices
Aye, aye.

Franklin
We are all proscribed now, Jefferson, you've heard the news.
(*Jefferson looks at him.*)
The king has issued abroad his list, and you and I and Washington are at the top. We are to be hanged first.

Sam Adams
(*Proudly.*)
I'm to be hanged too. It says so.

John Adams
(*Somewhat seriously.*)
So may we all be in time. You too, Sherman, Livingston. Being members of this committee seals the fact.

Jefferson

(*As he stares at the picture in his hand.*)
But as it says in the song, wait till ever the play is played. The king must take us first.

Sam Adams

Aye, and he shall taste our powder and ball and feel the hot point of our bayonets in his liver—that he shall in plenty.

Franklin

You're a man of flesh, Sam Adams, and I feel no pity for you. It's lean men like Jefferson here I regret—when the hanging comes.
    (*Cracking his joke.*)
Only yesterday I said to Richard Henry Lee and my old friend George Wythe, they of the light poundage—and John Dickinson likewise, I said—look to your bones, gentlemen. What? saith Gentleman George. Verily—and that quickly, I said. Put flesh on thy bones. Flesh is ye great cushioner against pain. Therefore eat heartily. Put flesh on thy bones, for a fat man ends quick when they hang him on high. Ye thin man suffers and struggles long, so 'tis said. True, true, saith Big Ben Harrison, standing by—who weighs twenty stone if a pound—And I shall be drinking the honeyed pots and mead of paradise long before you gentlemen arrive, he said. Ha-ha-ha.
    (*Chuckling and striking the table with his cane again.*)
So may my death be quick and easy.

Livingston

(*Smilingly, yet affectionately.*)
Before that should happen, sir, twice ten thousand sons of liberty will die in your defense.

Franklin

(*Warmly.*)
Spoken like a man, sir—
(*Soberly.*)
—a young man.
(*He takes out his steel-rimmed spectacles and puts them on.*)

Sam Adams

(*With a gesture of apology behind Franklin's back.*)
It's the wine. He drank too much.

Franklin

(*Turning on him jocularly.*)
You're a liar, Sam Adams. You yourself should drink a gill now and then. It might loosen the puritan shackles from your magnificent brain.
(*He smiles at Sam Adams with kind joshingness.*)
And now where are we?
(*Jefferson lays aside the picture and picks up his manuscript.*)

Jefferson

(*Sinking back into his seat.*)
I'm not satisfied with the preamble.

John Adams

The preamble's all right to me.

Others

It is.

JEFFERSON

(*Lifting off a sheet of paper and reading.*)
We hold these truths to be self-evident—that all men are endowed by their creator with inherent and inalienable rights, that among these are life, liberty and property.
(*Staring at the page.*)
I have changed that somewhat.
(*Reading again.*)
We hold these truths to be self-evident—
(*Hesitating, then firmly.*)
That all men are created equal, that they are endowed by their creator with inherent and inalienable rights.

FRANKLIN

Huh!

JOHN ADAMS

Equality—your Virginia aristocrats will jump on that.

JEFFERSON

The other statement was weak.

SAM ADAMS

Good, it's good.

LIVINGSTON

Men are not created equal.

SHERMAN

(*Chuckling.*)
I have a number of workmen there in Connecticut—each one different. One has so much money, another has so much. One is energetic—another lazy. How can they be equal?

Jefferson

(*Almost passionately.*)
I mean equal in humanity, equal in personal worth, in rights, in justice before the law and fair play and opportunity for their talents—their rights as men.

Sam Adams

He means equal in the soul.

Franklin

(*To John Adams.*)
Your cousin knows how to hit the nail on the head—let it stand. It will be debated and beaten to a frazzle in congress anyway.

Jefferson

(*Reading.*)
Life, liberty, and property. I don't like the word property.

Franklin

Saint's mercy, man, what's wrong with property! That's the heart of our subject.

Voices

It is.

Livingston

Government is instituted because of property. Our whole trouble with the king has been because of property.

Jefferson

When our men go marching into battle to pour out their life's blood—they won't do it for property. It'll be for something else—a principle they cherish beyond it. So here, when I write life, liberty and property—well, property seems less ideal after the other two.

Sherman

I say keep "property." We need a practical touch to this document.

Franklin

We out-vote you, Jefferson. Property it is.

Jefferson

I insist on the section concerning slavery.
    (*Reading.*)
Determined to keep open the market where *men* should be bought and sold he—the king—has prostituted his negative for suppressing every legislative attempt to prohibit or restrain this execrable commerce.

Franklin

    (*Smiling.*)
Now you accuse the king of that too.

Jefferson

I do.

John Adams

It's an inflammable matter. Let's forego it.

Sam Adams

It's good, good.

Livingston

We won't get anywhere on the subject of slavery. You might as well leave it out, Jefferson.

FRANKLIN

(*Chuckling.*)
New England has made money out of the slave trade. Your Virginia and the South raise their crops of tobacco with slave labor. Yes, leave it out.

JEFFERSON

(*Intensely.*)
But it must be dealt with sometime, somewhere. What time, what place better than now—here? Is this to be a declaration of fair and equitable principles or is it not?

SAM ADAMS

Jefferson is right. It's good.

FRANKLIN

(*Mockingly.*)
Good! Good!
(*To Jefferson.*)
But it's not expedient.

LIVINGSTON

Not practical.

JEFFERSON

(*Doggedly.*)
And I go on to say here—that after a certain day—and not too long off—the emancipation of the slaves shall begin—
(*There are exclamations of astonishment among the group.*)
—looking toward the ultimate freedom of them all.

VOICES

Free the slaves! Impossible!

JEFFERSON

(*Glancing at Sam Adams*)
Slaves are human beings, are they not? And to be a human being is to deserve the rights of citizenship. This document is being written for citizens—free citizens—irrespective of race, color, calling or creed.

FRANKLIN

A sweet alliteration. Daggers and blades, man, you *are* a fiery radical! George Wythe told me you were so—when you were his student there at the College of William and Mary.

JEFFERSON

Mr. Wythe taught me much. And in his name I thank you.

FRANKLIN

And bullheaded besides.
 (*Rising.*)
I too was young once—and hoped to save the world in a day. But still I admire you—even when you fail.

JEFFERSON

Fail?

FRANKLIN

Come, gentlemen. Or he'll never finish this document. Let him put in what he wishes about slavery. Congress will vote it out.

SAM ADAMS

Jefferson is right.
 (*Jefferson looks his tired and grateful thanks. Sam Adams goes on vehemently.*)

We'll fight 'em—fight Congress the way we'll fight the king—for the right, for the truth!
> (*He clenches his fist high in the air, then grabs Jefferson's hand fervently.*)

Franklin

We have a midnight function at Madam Dickinson's. We've got to go out there and cheer honest John up. This declaration is killing him. Come.
> (*He leads them off, twirling his cane. Just as they get outside, he stops and turns back into the room to Jefferson.*)

You may have heard—it was decided today. I am to sail to France at the earliest possible date.

Jefferson

Thank God! If any man can put the alliance through, it is you, Mr. Franklin.

Franklin

I'll do my best. I'll need your prayers.

Jefferson

You shall have them, sir.
> (*Franklin turns jauntily to his group and leads them off at the left.*)

The Group

(*Raising their song again.*)
   And we'll spit in old King George's eye,
   With a fa-la-la-la-la-la-la—
(*The men disappear at the left, and the singing gradually dies away with Franklin's voice in the*

lead. In the room Jefferson sits wearily down again with his manuscript on his lap. He gazes ahead of him in the air. Presently he picks up his pen and slowly resumes writing. The words are evoked through the narrator as before in a huge whisper.)

Narrator

(From the darkness, as Jefferson writes.)
Prudence indeed will dictate that nations long established—
  (Correcting as before.)
—governments long established—should not be changed for light and transient reasons—
  (Correcting.)
—causes—and accord-ing-ly—
  (The word begins repeating itself like a phonograph record.)
—accord-ing-ly—accord-ing-ly—
  (Jefferson's head sags over a bit in weariness. He shakes his shoulders and straightens up, knocking over the little picture on the table as he does so. He picks up the picture and gazes at it, his face filling with hunger and longing for his distant wife.)

Jefferson

(Impetuously, yearningly.)
Patty!
  (Softly the organ begins intensifying his mood of weariness, struggle and thoughts of home. The light slowly dims down on him and rises on the right rear center stage in a little nook, disclosing as a bit of inset interlude scene the corner of a room in Monticello—almost as if seen behind a gauze—as Jefferson sees it in his imagination. Here like a vision in a

dream a beautiful, frail young woman, Patty Jefferson, is seated at a harpsichord softly playing and singing. She is dressed in a light gown and bright-patterned night robe of the period. As she sings, her thoughts are going piteously across the void of seven hundred miles to her husband as his are flowing to her.)

Patty Jefferson

(The organ softly accompanying her.)

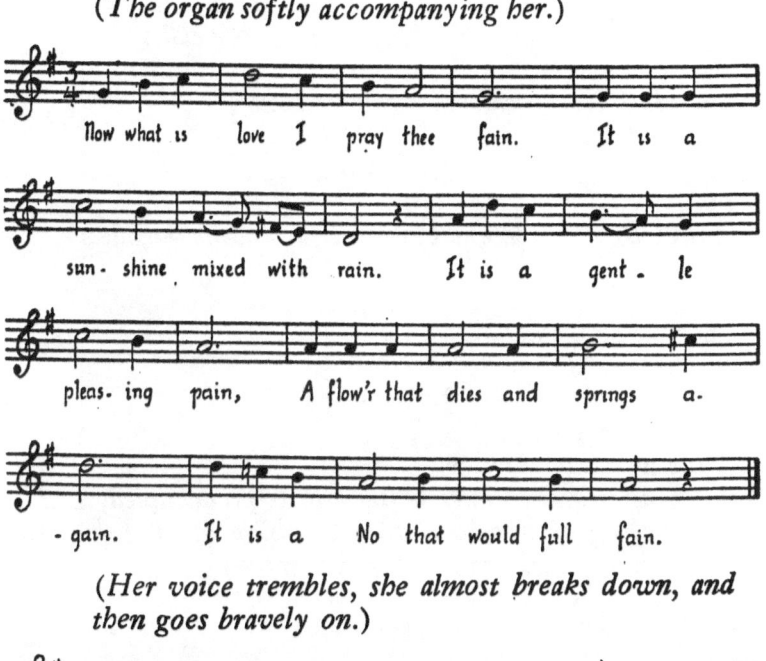

(Her voice trembles, she almost breaks down, and then goes bravely on.)

(At this moment the dim figures of Hugh Taylor and Sergeant Jack come striding in on the stage be-

fore the boardinghouse at the left front. They are both in uniform and are armed—Hugh with a sword at his waist and Sergeant Jack carrying a long rifle. They stop in the shadow, and Hugh calls out quietly.)

Hugh

Mr. Jefferson.
(*The light fades from the little inset scene at the right rear and comes up on Jefferson in the room. He is now leaning over, his head resting sleepily and heavily on the table. Hugh repeats the call.*)
Mr. Jefferson.
(*Jefferson gradually straightens up.*)

Jefferson

Yes.
(*Hugh goes in and Sergeant Jack waits outside.*)

Hugh

Your pardon, I'm late.

Jefferson

(*Abstractedly.*)
Come in, Hugh Taylor.
(*Jefferson's manner is still a little preoccupied, as if the fog of weariness and the vision of his beloved wife still lurk shadowly in his brain.*)

Hugh

I came for the letters, sir.
(*He looks at Jefferson appraisingly.*)

Jefferson

Yes.

Hugh

Our ammunition wagons are loaded at last and we're starting back for Virginia by dawn.
  (*Jefferson shakes his head now awake.*)

Jefferson

(*Murmuring.*)
Ammunition—good. We'll need it—plenty of it.
  (*He pulls open a drawer of the table and takes out a little packet, and turns to Hugh.*)
Cherish these letters with your life, Hugh. And for heaven's sake, as soon as you get to Williamsburg, see that they are hurried off to my wife at Monticello.

Hugh

I will, sir.

Jefferson

The last I heard from her was four weeks ago.
  (*He sighs.*)
She is very frail.
  (*He throws out his hands dolefully.*)
Ah—
  (*Looking up at Hugh.*)
There will come a time, Hugh Taylor, when the doctors will know something. Now the curse of this land is the death of our infants—flies, mosquitoes, heat, bad food. We know nothing. The doctors cut and bleed and practice their barbarism. And our loved ones die!
  (*Gazing ahead of him burningly.*)
But someday men will know.

Hugh

Aye.

JEFFERSON

Ah, a man needs to live a thousand years—before wisdom will come to him.
>(*Jefferson's spirits obviously have been cast down, like any sensitive artist, by the visit of the committee of criticism. He rubs his forehead heavily as if to iron away a pain there.*)

HUGH

You ought to rest, Mr. Jefferson. You've been cooped up here for days—writing, writing.

JEFFERSON

Merciful goodness! How can I rest. This document's due in congress on Monday.
>(*Striking the table with his fist.*)

And it's not finished, I can't seem to get it right.

HUGH

What you read to me last night was right.

JEFFERSON

It seems dead and dull. The committee's just been here. And if men like Franklin and John Adams can't see the truth—how can I expect—?
>(*Shaking his head.*)

Sam Adams saw it. But then he's a fanatic and has little influence in congress.

HUGH

That part about equality is the truth. I know.
>(*His hand on his breast.*)

In here—a man can feel it—and men will so feel it everywhere, and fight for it.

JEFFERSON

Property, they say, is the basis of our dream. I fear congress will agree.

HUGH

Property is important enough all right—when you haven't got it.

JEFFERSON

But the principle we're after is so much bigger.

HUGH

My family had no property—so I know its value. My father died a hireling on the great Gordon plantation—his life an empty pursuit of happiness he never found—his children hewers of wood and drawers of water.

JEFFERSON

And in your pride as a man you fled from it.
(*With sudden musingness.*)
"Pursuit of happiness"—an apt phrase, Hugh.

HUGH

Aye, fled from its bondage and slavery.
(*He throws out his hands.*)

JEFFERSON

The committee fails me there too—slavery.
(*Angrily as if quoting.*)
Not practical, not expedient to abolish it. But someday it must be—even if through blood.

Hugh

My father had no rights as a citizen. He was not even allowed the vote—Aye, a slave.

(*Mockingly.*)

Are you a free-holder? No. Stand aside. You don't count. And that's why I say—let the war come—and I will fight in it—fight for the freedom that belongs to me and which my father never had. A man's got to have his own things, Mr. Jefferson, have the right to get them, the opportunity to do it—just the way he has a right in here—

(*He hits his breast.*)

—to have his own religion and faith in his own God.

Jefferson

True, true.

(*A touch of jubilancy in his weary face for an instant.*)

It's for you, Hugh Taylor, and men like you I write this declaration—the real American.

Hugh

And it's for Americans everywhere to measure up to what you write. I pray God you will stand firm against them all, Mr. Jefferson.

(*As his face relaxes a bit.*)

You see, I've read all your writings.

(*He sticks out his hand. Jefferson rises and takes it warmly—a grip of man to man. They are of about the same height and look into each other's eyes with a deep and manly understanding.*)

Jefferson

Convey my regards to stern Cousin Robert and his daughter, the lovely Eileen when you see them.—How is she?

Hugh

Well.

Jefferson

Not married.
>(*Hugh shakes his head, nervously stuffing the packet of letters inside his blouse.*)

Young Corbin has not carried her off yet?

Hugh

No.

Jefferson

And so in the war you can fight for your love as well as happiness.

Hugh

>(*Abruptly.*)

Good night, sir.

Jefferson

Good night, and God bless you. I'll see you soon in Williamsburg.
>(*Hugh turns and goes swiftly out, and he and Sergeant Jack move away in the darkness at the left. Jefferson gazes after them a moment, then turns quickly back to his seat, picks up his pen and bends over his manuscript, writing. He lifts the manuscript and reads a bit of it appraisingly but energetically. Once more the words he reads are evoked through the narrator.*)

Narrator

>(*In his huge whisper.*)

We hold these truths to be self-evident—that all men are created equal—that they are endowed by their creator with certain inalienable rights. That among these are life, liberty and—the pursuit of happiness.

(He resumes his writing swiftly. The light dies out and comes up again on the narrator.)

Narrator

In a few days Jefferson finished his Declaration and it was laid before congress. Parts of it were cut out as the wise Benjamin Franklin had prophesied and parts of it were amended. It was finally passed by unanimous vote on July 4, 1776. The news spread rapidly from province to province. Bells were rung and celebrations were held. The people in Williamsburg were filled with joy and pride and justly so, for this little town had mothered most of the great men whose ideas had led to this event. When Jefferson arrived home the people turned out to welcome him here with flags and cheers. And the newly-elected governor, Patrick Henry, read the great document to the welcoming throng. And even our old friend Cephus Sicklemore, who had been hiding away from service in the army, appeared on the scene.

(The light fades from the narrator and comes up on the center stage.)

SCENE 7

The Duke of Gloucester Street in Williamsburg, the village green behind, and in the distance the red chimneys and gleaming weather vane of the governor's palace. The little courthouse is in the center rear and here in front of it and along the street a concourse of people is assembled, making a gay picture with their varicolored dress—artisans, working people, aristocrats—elderly, middle-aged and young—men and women, a few patriot soldiers and a gaudy Cherokee Indian chief and a number of his full-panoplied braves. The occasion is a festive one, and the scene is decorated with red, white and blue bunting. And the new Virginia flag is in plentiful evidence—a few big ones held aloft and many of the people carrying little ones in their hands.

As if ushering the scene into illuminated distinctness, the organ plays a swift-running bit of music, underneath which sounds the growl and boomp of distant guns.

Standing on the porch of the courthouse, surrounded by his admiring fellow citizens, is the matchless Patrick Henry. Thomas Jefferson is standing somewhat in the background with the Reverend Mr. Madison and Hugh Taylor. Great actor and colorful figure, Henry is in the

zenith of his magnificence. He is gloriously dressed for the day and in keeping with his office in a sumptuous scarlet cloak, dark velvet clothes and great wig.

The people are waving and cheering, stimulated somewhat by the swirl of organ phrase. Henry has stopped an instant in his reading. He is near the conclusion of it and holds the document aloft in his hand, the other hand praying in the air as it were—"your forbearance, your gentle attention, friends, patriots, fellow citizens all." Tears are streaming down his face. He is in an almost ecstatic state of fervency. Some of the people are weeping too and wiping their eyes even as they wave and cheer him. All have their faces lifted glowingly toward the great orator.

Henry

(*His voice soaring aloft, his hawk-like face illumined with his inner passion.*)
We therefore, the representatives of—
  (*He pauses just the exact and necessary instant of time for dramatic emphasis, then spills over in an underscoring stridency of the next few words.*)
—the United States—of—America!
  (*He pauses and applause breaks out again. His hand prays for indulgence.*)
—In general congress assembled, appealing to the supreme judge of the world—
  (*He turns his gleaming eye for an instant upward toward the divine ruler of the universe.*)
—for the rectitude of our intentions—do in the name and by the authority of—the—
  (*Hesitating and then shooting the dynamic word out.*)
—people—of these colonies—
  (*Repeating.*)

—do in the name and by the authority of the good people of these colonies solemnly publish and declare that these—
   (*Again the proper rhythm and emotionally drenched delivery.*)
—United Colonies—
   (*Cheers and applause for the word "united."*)
—United Colonies are and of right ought to be—
   (*He fires the next few words volley-like into the air.*)
—free and independent states!
   (*The people break loose in wild cheering, and the organ sends forth its feeling, simulating in its depths once more the distant booming of guns.*)

PEOPLE

'Ray, 'Ray! Freedom! Freedom!

OTHER PEOPLE

(*Whistling and shouting.*)
Patrick Henry! Patrick Henry!

STILL OTHERS

Thomas Jefferson! Jefferson forever! Jefferson!
   (*Two or three little boys as if energized by the evangelism of the scene run out from the crowd and begin turning cartwheels and leaping around like*

*volatile and spasmodic frogs. Henry's spirit is one
with the people. He bows to the right and to the
left. Then he puts out his hands again, begging
the population for attention. Instantly the air grows
still. Two mothers, one of them Mammy Huzzitt,
come out and grab their little sons by their coat
collars and march them back into the crowd.)*

Henry

(His voice riding high and triumphant.)
That they are absolved from all allegiance to the British
crown, and that all political connection between them
and the state of Great Britain is—
*(Once more the matchless appraiser of the people's
emotions, he holds the words in the air.)*
—and ought to be totally dissolved—
(The applause breaks out again.)
—that as free and independent states—
(His words rushing on.)
—they have full power to levy war, conclude peace, contract alliances, establish commerce—
*(His face is working with emotion and his words
are running like a song now, accompanied by wide-spaced and low chords from the organ.)*
—and to do all other actions and things which independent states may have right to do.
*(He lowers his hand and folds up the document. He
has memorized the rest of the Declaration, and as
he stows the foolscap away in his coat his bent
shoulders straighten up, his face is swept with a look
of humility and piety, and he delivers the final
words with the lyric power which has for years
made him a household word throughout the colonies.)*

—And for the support of this Declaration, with firm reliance on the protection of divine providence—

(*Once more with a glance of his eyes upward he reiterates the adoration which flows from him to man's divine author and creator in the sky. Then after this the tones of his voice grow firmer, almost harsh, almost defiant.*)

—we mutually pledge to each other, our lives—

(*Comment from the organ.*)

—our fortunes—

(*Again the organ.*)

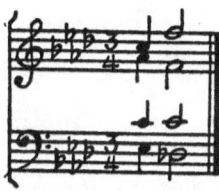

—and our sacred honor!

(*His hands are now raised high above him. He stands on his tiptoe as if reaching to illustrate his feeling for the honor he calls sacred.*)

126   THE COMMON GLORY

VOICES

(*Roaring as the distant guns boom and the organ plays.*)
Patrick Henry! Patrick Henry!
(*The great orator unashamedly wipes his face with his newly-tailored sleeve.*)

OTHER VOICES

The United Colonies! Thomas Jefferson!
(*Henry with a swift motion of his hand unsheathes his great saber and holds it gleaming above him, apparently ready to cut down any who might rise to oppose him. As if pricking an object high in the air, he lunges forward and gestures the people into another cheer.*)

HENRY, JEFFERSON AND THE PEOPLE

'Ray! 'Ray! 'Ray!

HENRY

(*Roaring out.*)
And now—music!
(*Turning to the rear and applauding.*)
Miss Hallam! Miss Hallam!
(*The organ, moved by the fervor of the occasion, strikes up a dance. Miss Hallam runs down from the portico and leads the people in a country dance. The dance continues for a moment with the soldiers and the other people clapping their hands and joining in.*)

THE COMMON GLORY

(*While the dance is going full fervor and the chorus adding its la-la-la with the melody and clapping hands also, Cephus Sicklemore comes stepping circumspectly and hungrily in at the right rear. He is in rather foul and piteous condition from scattered back-door pickings and sleepings in tavern yards at night. He suddenly catches sight of two patriot soldiers coming behind him and lopes over toward the right front of the scene to escape. But there he is met by two other patriot soldiers, one of them Sergeant Jack. He whirls back, the soldiers closing in on him. He stretches out his hands to the people to help him— to save him from the army. They ignore him. He turns pleadingly to Mammy Huzzitt but she shies away and goes on clapping her hands. The soldiers now have him down on his knees. One of them prods him in the rear with a musket and he leaps to his feet with a soundless howl. A gun is shoved into his stomach, then into his hands. He takes it finally and stands there, a shaking half-weeping hulk. The dance builds to a climax and then winds up on a long drawn chord of the organ, the people hot and happy. But the dancing is not ended. For suddenly the Indians let loose a volley of yells, and led by the grandiose chief, spring out into the middle of the scene and begin going it in a spectacular tribal dance, depicting their friendship and alliance with the white man. They turn, cavort, twist and leap, striking their breasts with their fists, flinging their palms outward and reaching their arms into the air in a pantomime of embracing. The crowd of people look on with admiration and loud delight, and the organ joins joyously in with its drumbeat.*)

(*The dance concludes. The people applaud, and the Indians return proudly to their place. Patrick Henry now resumes command of the scene. His lyric voice soars out again.*)

Henry

And so today, my friends, my countrymen—and our new brave allies and comrades—
   (*He indicates the chief and his warriors. The chief bows deeply.*)
—we gather here and in our festivities honor the immortal words—of the Declaration of Independence.
   (*He slaps his breast resoundingly with the flat of his hand where the document resides. The people are now still as death, as if in a church or standing before an altar.*)
And we honor the man who wrote these words—
   (*Turning.*)
Thomas Jefferson!
   (*He ushers him forward. The people cheer and the organ booms out its repeating flourish of announcement and praise.*)

People

(*Led by Henry.*)
'Ray! 'Ray! Jefferson! Jefferson!

(Jefferson looks out at the people, his face full of deep feeling. They grow quiet. He speaks in the simplest and most sincere manner as the people wait breathlessly on every word.)

JEFFERSON

Our great Virginian, Patrick Henry, has glowingly pictured to you the purpose of this war. I have returned here to help with all my strength in fighting that war. And in truth—what are we fighting for—what does this flag stand for?

(He indicates the Virginia flag being held by a soldier close by.)

We are fighting for a free earth—an earth that belongs to you and to your sons and their sons and not to the few and powerful. For the right to pass our own laws as becomes honest men. For the right to speak freely and unafraid the thoughts that are in us. For the freedom of the written word—that we may publish forth these thoughts unafraid. For the right to use the fruits of our labor for our own happiness and welfare and not for potentates and kings. Fighting for the right to our own religion—the inner life of the spirit—not to be controlled by outward authorities and rules; yes, freedom of religion. Fighting that there shall be no persecution of a man, no taxation on a man, no penalty because of his belief in his own God and in his own worship as he feels them to be in his own soul. For the right of education for all the people, the high and the low, to drink from the fountain of knowledge freely. We are fighting, my friends, for self-government, for the eradication forever of all dictatorship over us as free and self-reliant men.

(*Slowly and impressively.*)

And that means—meeting hardships and sufferings unafraid, a willingness to endure them, taking the blows and the buffetings for the cause in which we believe.

(*Cephus straightens up a bit and seems to be listening.*)

And I repeat a solemn warning. Let no man dissuade himself, let no man be blinded to the truth. A heavy and bloody struggle lies ahead of us. Today we are calling for men, today we are calling for women—calling for consecration of character, of stamina—that these principles may live! And the government based on them can be only as strong as our devotion to them. This is not to be a government of a few people, but of all the people.

(*His voice still quiet, but intense and burning.*)

These are the things we must fight for, these are the things for which many of us, the living here today, must die. And the struggle to make these principles prevail shall be the common glory of us all. And now we cry "to arms"—and into the hands of Almighty God commend us!

(*He steps back to his former position.*)

Henry

We will proceed forthwith to Bruton Church—to pray for divine guidance in our cause.

(*During Jefferson's last words Cephus has seemed to pay close attention, and his sagging form has grown even a little less bent and enervated. Young Reverend Mr. Madison steps forward, his hands outstretched.*)

132   THE COMMON GLORY

MR. MADISON

(*Fervently.*)
We will lift up our eyes unto the hills
From whence cometh our strength.
Our help cometh even from the Lord.

PEOPLE

(*In a great answering unison.*)
Who hath made heaven and earth.

ALL

(*Chanting as the organ accompanies.*)

(*While the chant continues, Henry, Jefferson, Reverend Mr. Madison and those on the steps of the courthouse move down, led by a soldier bearing the huge Virginia flag. The rest of the people fall in behind them. The procession moves to the right, the chant growing in power, aided now by the chorus joining in from the darkness.*)

THE COMMON GLORY

PEOPLE AND CHORUS

(*In a great uplifting harmony.*)

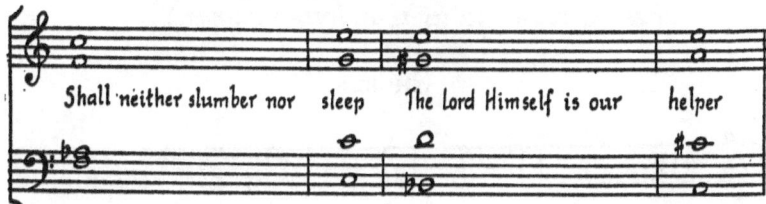

Shall neither slumber nor sleep The Lord Himself is our helper

The Lord is our de-fence Upon our right hand I will lift up mine

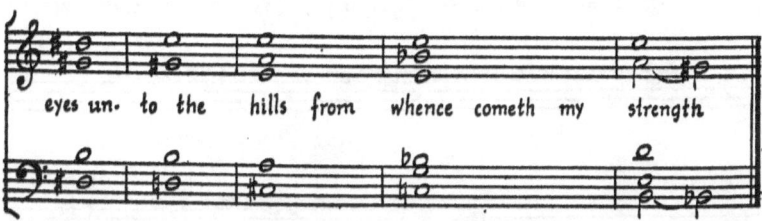

eyes un-to the hills from whence cometh my strength.

(*As the people march away, the Indians move with them and the group of soldiers comes last. At a gesture from the sergeant, Cephus takes his place in the ranks, still hesitant and uncertain. But as the chant increases in power he puts his musket on his shoulder and joins the tail-end of the procession and lifts his head up, even a bit proudly—for now Mammy Huzzitt's two little boys are marching along with him, looking up at him, their little forms almost popping at the seams with pride.*)

THE COMMON GLORY

The light fades away from the center stage and comes up on the left side stage where the chorus is now standing in a full blaze of light. The mighty chant is raised to its thundering climax.)

CHORUS

Glory be to the Father and to the Son And to the Holy Ghost.

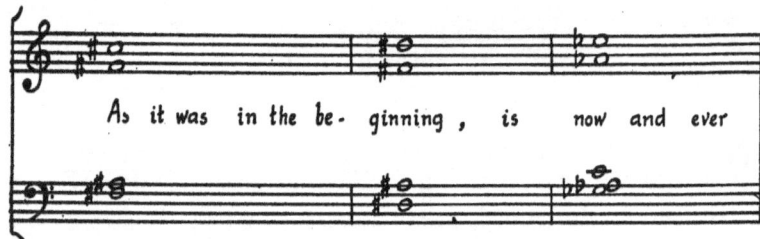

As it was in the be- ginning, is now and ever

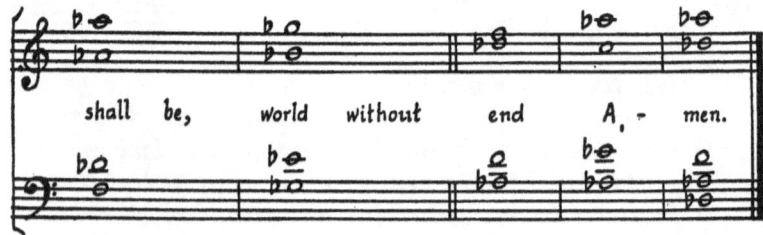

shall be, world without end A - men.

(The light dies out on the chorus and comes up in the theatre.)

INTERMISSION

Act Two

SCENE 1

After the intermission, the organist enters his box and begins the overture. When the audience is assembled, and at a signal in the music, the lights begin to go down, and the chorus enters its stall up and behind the left side stage. The light dies out from both the organist and the audience and comes up brightly on the choir as it stands and chants the Lord's prayer unaccompanied.

(The light fades from the chorus and comes up on the narrator.)

NARRATOR

And trusting in the help of Almighty God, the Old Dominion in confidence and hope went forth to war. With men like Thomas Jefferson and Patrick Henry to guide her she faced the future unafraid. And while his associates strove to beat back the enemy on the field of battle, Jefferson flung himself wholeheartedly into waging an even harder battle here in Williamsburg—to get established into the laws of the new commonwealth the principles for which this war was being fought. And with few exceptions, notably the one on religious freedom, the legislature voted his reforms into the structure of the legal code. Finally after almost two years of arduous labor his task was finished.

But now an even heavier task fell upon him. Patrick Henry's health had failed under the strain, and Virginia called upon Jefferson to become her military head and second governor. Unflinchingly and at great personal sacrifice, he assumed that responsibility. Once more he demonstrated his dynamic leadership. And everywhere throughout the commonwealth the people answered his call. The women wove and spun and knitted and carded for the cause as long as cotton or wool could be got. And the ladies of Williamsburg tore up the last of their fine petticoats for bandages.

(The organ breaks into the melody, "Heart of Oak," and the light dims down on the narrator and rises on the side stage at the left in the first of a series of montage scenes.)

Action A

A group of some ten or a dozen women, young, middle-aged and old, are revealed working away, preparing bandages. They sing energetically and almost merrily "la-la" in time to the music as they work. The action is all in pantomime. Two or three of the women carry on the swift motions of sewing with their needles. Others are rolling up bandages, and another is sitting twirling her spinning wheel. A young soldier with an open tow sack is standing in the scene, and two of the women are packing bandages and supplies into it. The light dies out from the scene and remains dimmed down on the narrator. We hear his voice again.

Narrator

The farmers gave of their threshings and reapings, their cattle and their stock.

(The light holds dimly on the narrator and comes up brightly on the side stage at the right.)

Action B

Here we see a farmer pantomiming the pouring of grain from a piggin into a sack held by a young soldier. Half-hidden behind them are three young women treading barefooted up and down in the pantomime of threshing grain, their skirts held above their ankles. A boy crouched near by is flailing away in the pantomime of threshing likewise. All of these are humming to the music in the organ. The light fades out from the scene and the narrator speaks again.

Narrator

And the blacksmiths and the merchants, the fishermen and boatmen likewise gave to their uttermost.

Action C

The light comes up in a nook on the left forestage. Here we see a smith with his sweaty sleeves rolled up beating a red-hot horseshoe into shape on an anvil. A boy is pumping a bellows behind him. Close by a mechanic seated on a drum of wood is working at a gun. Another man is sharpening a sabre over a grindstone which is being turned by a second boy. The hammer of the blacksmith does not actually strike the anvil nor does the sabre touch the grindstone. These motions are pantomime only. The men are all humming in heavy and bass-filled unison to the music as they work. The light fades from the scene, and once more the narrator speaks.

Narrator

And even in the iron mines the workers and convicts swung their picks as if glimpsing the new day of freedom waiting there ahead.

140   THE COMMON GLORY

Action D

The light comes up in a burning, almost horizontal shaft of sun across the center stage at the rear. The organ music stops. Some eight or ten convicts in line and stripped to the waist are swinging their picks—digging rhythmically across the scene, from left to right. Two motionless guards with muskets are standing at either end of the line of diggers. As the convicts swing their picks, their sweaty torsos gleaming in the light, the voice of the narrator speaks now from the darkness.

Narrator

(*With the picks coming down.*)
Dig this iron—hanh!
(*The organ comments.*)

Narrator

Dig this iron—hanh!
(*Comment from the organ again. The convicts dig on. The sympathetic chorus lifts its voice in loud harmony.*)

Chorus

(*In unison.*)

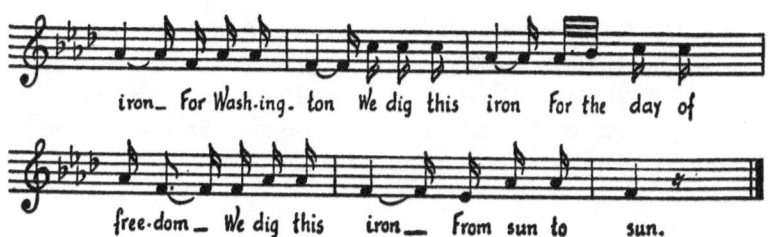

iron— For Wash-ing-ton We dig this iron for the day of free-dom— We dig this iron— From sun to sun.

(*The digging increases in fervor and splurge. A tenor soloist in the chorus gives vent to his feeling.*)

Voice

'Way up on the moun-tain Heard my sav-iour say Trial and tri-bu-la-tion cru-ci-fy my way.

Narrator

Dig this iron—hanh! Dig this iron—hanh!

(*The light fades slowly out on the scene and the narrator's voice diminishes with it down to a low, husky whisper.*)

Dig this iron—hanh.

(*The light on the center stage dies into the darkness and comes up again full on the narrator as he speaks.*)

Work, work, produce, produce, arms and supplies, ever more supplies, and always men, men. But this was never enough, no matter how much was furnished it was never enough. And the news that kept coming back from the north was bad. Washington was forever retreating, his forces weak and poorly armed. And from the south it was the same. Savannah fell, Charleston was threatened, and the British power slowly began reaching its way northward toward Virginia. And along the roads everywhere piteous was the spectacle of sick and wounded and crippled soldiers returning home.

Action E

The light comes up on the front part of the center stage, this time an almost horizontal shaft, dawn cold and funereal as contrasted with the former light of the burning sun. The chorus begins a low lamenting and pleading chant.

Chorus

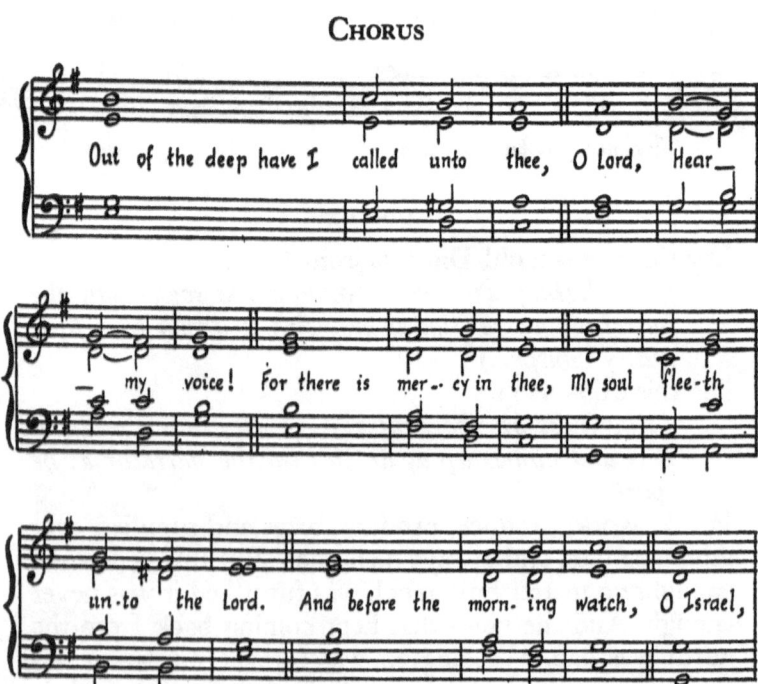

Out of the deep have I called unto thee, O Lord, Hear my voice! For there is mercy in thee, My soul fleeth unto the Lord. And before the morning watch, O Israel,

THE COMMON GLORY 143

Coming in from the right and moving toward the source of light almost like figures in a dream is a sorrowful home-seeking group of wounded and sick soldiers. Some of them are walking with the aid of crutches or cudgels, and some are helped along by their more fortunate comrades. Here and there in the gloom a bandage is seen, wrapped around a man's face or forehead. As they shuffle and tramp across the scene there come now and then from their lips the dry gusty mumbles and moans of pain in rhythm to the chorus lament to which their bruised feet are treading. We discern Hugh Taylor there and also Cephus. The narrator speaks forth some of the words of the chant as well as the pleadings of the marchers.

Narrator

(*Above the chorus.*)
Out of the deep—have I called unto thee. Have mercy Lord—Lord, have mercy!

(*Now come two fellows carrying a crude stretcher on which a soldier is lying with pale, upturned lolling head. A group of refugees appears—an old woman, a husband and wife with little children, and their belongings tied in crude bundles. The narrator goes on.*)

Home—home— Help us— O help us!

(*A sick man collapses. Hugh and Cephus help lift him to his feet and onward. The procession continues dolorously on across and out at the other side of the stage. The music dies away and the light comes up on the narrator.*)

Narrator

And daily the patriot cause grew gloomier and gloomier. But ever unyielding, ever working ahead, Jefferson kept sending troops and supplies as they could be collected—writing letters endlessly to Washington, to Gates, to Greene and Thomas Nelson. But finally the strain on Virginia reached the point of exhaustion. A reaction against the governor set in—and a spirit of disunion and criticism spread even into the house of delegates.

(*The light fades from the narrator and comes up on the left side stage.*)

SCENE 2

An inner office room in the governor's palace. The architecture and furnishings are beautiful in their symmetry and color. Jefferson is seated in the middle of the room at a table loaded with papers and documents. Standing before him in respectful attention is a crusty middle-aged infantry captain. At a writing desk to the right a young boy clerk about fifteen or sixteen years old sits sagged over, an ink bottle and several quill pens and sheets of letter paper in front of him. He is groggy from work and sleeplessness. Over to the left of the desk are a harpsichord and a chair.

JEFFERSON
(*Continuing.*)
I have drawn a map here showing the best route. March by Hobbs Hole, thence turn by way of Fredericksburg. The ferry over the Rappahannock is threatened by a Tory band.

CAPTAIN
Yes, sir.

JEFFERSON
You should get these men to General Washington in six days.

CAPTAIN
(*Incredulously.*)
Six days!

JEFFERSON
Six days. They must be in marching order and leave Williamsburg tomorrow at dawn. At any moment Clinton is likely to start his offensive.

CAPTAIN

I'll do my best, sir, but the men—

JEFFERSON

(*Almost bitterly.*)
I know, the men are ill-clad, their shoes poor. And they must spend Christmas Day marching on the road.
(*Picking up a paper and shooting it out at him.*)
I know, I know.

CAPTAIN

Yes, sir.
(*He salutes and turns away.*)

JEFFERSON

I will come and speak to them before they leave.

CAPTAIN

(*Heartily.*)
It will help, sir.
(*He goes away at the right front. Jefferson picks up a letter and turns toward his clerk. The boy shakes his shoulders and straightens up.*)

JEFFERSON

(*Kindly.*)
You've been at these letters for five straight hours. Well, another one or two and you may go for tonight.
(*The boy dips his pen into the inkstand, hides a terrific yawn, and Jefferson begins dictating.*)
Williamsburg—and date—To General George Washington, Commander-in-Chief, the American forces, Morristown, New Jersey. Your Excellency. With you and likewise the Committee of Congress I am mindful of the

grave danger now threatening our cause. I have moved with all expedition to fulfill your several requests. I regret that the results of my efforts in levy of men and arms must prove as disappointing to you as to myself. The county committees have most zealously—

> (*The door at the rear opens and Martha Carr, Jefferson's sister, appears. She is an efficient, strong and attractive widow of thirty or more. Jefferson glances up and starts to resume his letter.*)

MARTHA

Ever more working and writing.

JEFFERSON

Yes.

MARTHA

And that poor boy, almost dead in his chair.

JEFFERSON

What is it, sister mine?

MARTHA

> (*With a backward indication of her head.*)

Your passel of nieces and nephews want to come in.
> (*As Jefferson starts to object.*)

Mr. Wythe is taking them hobgobling in the town.
> (*Pointedly.*)

And your wife wants to speak to you.
> (*She turns back into the hall as old Aunt Nancy, a household Negro mammy and dressed accordingly and with a bright kerchief around her kinky nest of hair helps Patty Jefferson into the room. Mrs. Jeffer-*)

son carries a package in one hand, and with the other holds tremblingly to Aunt Nancy's arm. She is dressed in a becoming lacy house gown. The old Negress carries a drinking mug. Jefferson rises quickly and speaks up almost reprimandingly.)

JEFFERSON

Patty!
(He hurries to her solicitously.)

AUNT NANCY

Now, now, Massa Tom, just a minute or two and I'se gwine slap her right back into bed.

PATTY

(Somewhat pleadingly.)
It's Christmas Eve, my darling.
(Jefferson puts his arm helpingly around her. She smiles wanly up at him.)
And we always sing our carols—remember. The children count on it.

JEFFERSON

I was coming to your room later.

AUNT NANCY

Yes, suh, mebbe sunrise tomorrow morning when we'se ready to begin the new day.

JEFFERSON

I'll soon be through my work here, on my honor.

AUNT NANCY

You ain't got no honor where work is concerned. And here's your eggnog.
  (*Jefferson relinquishes Patty into the chair before the harpsichord. Her eager slim hand goes out and touches the keybord in a tinkle of notes. He takes the mug of eggnog and begins drinking it. He looks over the rim with smiling eyes at his wife.*)
Mis' Martha done had a big bait of that eggnog. She say it the best Randy ever made.

JEFFERSON

Wonderful! I will give him especial thanks.
  (*He turns to his little clerk.*)
You may go for awhile.
  (*The boy staggers to his feet and eagerly leaves the room—at the right front. Aunt Nancy drapes a shawl around Patty Jefferson's shoulders. Some five or six children of different sizes now come trooping in at the rear accompanied by George Wythe. They vary in ages from six or seven up to fifteen, some two or three boys and the rest girls. Their faces are hid in home-made masks somewhat like those children now wear at Halloween—made of cornshucks, bits of cloth, straw or what not, and one of them is a horned and hooved little devil in red. They are in hilarious spirits. Two or three of them carry lighted candles. George Wythe is a thin ascetic man past middle age and with a noble dome of bald head. He carries a lighted lantern, and a huge minotaur mask hangs in front of him at his waist. Martha comes in behind him.*)

WYTHE

Merry Christmas, Jefferson.

Jefferson

(*Genially as he sets aside his empty mug.*)
Merry Christmas, Mr. Wythe.
(*Indicating the mask.*)
And I see you're fixed for a frolic.

Wythe

And who would ever have thought it—a man of my age. But this comes from having these children around.
(*He holds up his mask. Martha stands gazing at the children in fond indulgence.*)

Children

(*Suddenly.*)
Boo! Boo!
(*Jefferson pretends to be frightened and hides behind his wife's chair. Patty likewise pretends.*)

Jefferson

(*Shivering.*)
Hoo, mercy on me, mercy!

Patty

You terrible creatures!
(*The children go into peals of laughter, each one thinking he is the most frightful thing imaginable.*)

Children

(*Hopping around Jefferson and chanting.*)
Christmas gif', Christmas gif'.

Jefferson

Not till tomorrow. Everybody gets his gift on Christmas Day.

WYTHE

We're going serenading through the town, Jefferson.

JEFFERSON

That's a deal of fun. We'd always do that at Monticello.
(He looks ahead of him, his tired face easing itself a bit in remembrance.)

WYTHE

Then we're going to sing carols at Bruton Church. We need your tenor.

PATTY

(As she holds his hand against her cheek.)
Please, you go with them.

JEFFERSON

No, no. I've got these—
(Then hurriedly.)
And now our carol.
(He pulls out his spectacles, puts them on and lifts a hymn book from the top of the harpsichord. The children line up in front of Jefferson, and Wythe takes his place behind them.)

MARTHA

(Almost spitefully.)
Aha—wearing spectacles at your age! Well, a blind husband and a—
(Stopping.)
What shall we sing?

TWO CHILDREN

(Ad lib, beggingly.)
"Adeste Fidelis, Adeste Fidelis."

152   THE COMMON GLORY

The Other Children

(*Ad lib loudly.*)
"Down in Yon Forest, Down in Yon Forest!"

Jefferson

The majority wins.
(*Pulling a pitch pipe from his pocket, he sounds an elfin note, and then sings the first line as he lays the hymn book aside.*)
"Down in yon forest be a hall,
   Sing May, Queen May, sing Mary,"
(*Patty begins to play. Jefferson lifts his hands beating time and the children begin singing, Wythe and Martha joining in.*)

All

(*Singing as Jefferson conducts them.*)

(*The bright chirrupy voices of the children rise in sweet harmony. Jefferson's face is filled with love and good cheer for a moment. Patty looks out happily at them all above the harpsichord.*)

Oh in that hall is a pallet bed:
'Tis stained with blood like cardinal red.

And at that pallet is a stone
On which the Virgin did atone.

Under that hall is a gushing flood:
From Christ's own side 'tis water and blood.

Beside that bed a shrub tree grows,
Since He was born hit blooms and blows.

(*The harmony sounds louder now as the chorus joins softly in from the stall at the left.*)

Oh, on that bed a young squire sleeps,
His wounds are sick, and see, he weeps.

Oh hail yon hall where none can sin,
Cause hit's gold outside and silver within.

(*They all wind up with a strong climax. Jefferson applauds them.*)

Jefferson

(*Beaming.*)
Splendid, wonderful.

Two or Three Children

(*Hopping about.*)
Merry Christmas.

Other Children

Christmas gif', Christmas gif'.

Martha

And now goodnight—
 (*Shooing them out.*)
Goodnight.

Wythe

Goodnight all.
 (*He kisses Patty's hand and turns toward the door, putting on his minotaur's mask and growling and looking ferocious as he goes. The children squeal at him.*)

Children

Whee-oo! Whee-oo!
 (*Then ad lib.*)
Goodnight, goodnight, Uncle Thomas.

Jefferson and Patty

Goodnight.

Jefferson

 (*To Wythe.*)
Be sure to give Edmund Pendleton a good frightening!

Wythe

 (*With right good feeling.*)
I'll see that we do, Jefferson.

Children

 (*Ad lib joyously.*)
We will, oh, we will.
 (*They tear out of the room at the rear with a scamper, Wythe and Martha following. Jefferson stares after them.*)

Patty

Those children love you like a father.

Jefferson

And I loved their father like—
>   (*Abruptly.*)

What a strength Dabney Carr would be in the cause now if he had lived!
>   (*He gestures.*)

Patty

And master George Wythe loves you like a son.
>   (*For a moment Jefferson stands looking before him, his great lean hands clasping and unclasping themselves.*)

There you go again—worrying, thinking.

Jefferson

Aye, aye.
>   (*He reaches out and touches her hair.*)

And now my lovely, off to bed with you.

Patty

And you'll sit up writing, writing. I forbid it.

Jefferson

To finish one letter, I promise you, to General Washington.

Patty

Well, to General Washington then.

Jefferson

Ah, Patty, what good fortune it is that this country takes its beginning under him. People have to have examples, images to go by. And the figure of Washington stands there as strong and self-reliant before us all. Every American hereafter can be better, more honest because of him. We will have him to copy after. Yes, I confess it, he is becoming a hero with me, and I believe in him.

Patty

You are my hero and I believe in you.
> (*He starts to help her across the room, but she stops and stands looking up at him, the package she had been holding in her lap now in her hands. She continues naively and with a slightly embarrassed girlish smile.*)

I've brought your Christmas present tonight.
> (*She opens the package and lifts out and holds up a pair of carpet slippers.*)

The floor is so cold and I know you need them now.

Jefferson

> (*Taking them.*)

They're beautiful.
> (*He looks at them a moment, hugs her to him and kisses her.*)

Patty

And warm. Sit right down now and put them on.
> (*She pushes at him, and obediently he sinks down in a chair, slides off his buckled low shoes and puts on the new slippers. Patty sits down on a foot stool near him.*)

I worked them all myself. A thousand stitches and every stitch a kiss.

JEFFERSON

(*Jocularly.*)
A man walking in kisses. I never heard of that before.

PATTY

(*Emphatically now, gazing sternly at him.*)
And each kiss is an order too, a fierce military command—to you, sir—to relax, to rest.

JEFFERSON

I do—now I do.
> (*He leans his head against her—then with deep contentment.*)

It seems I could rest a thousand years—here.

PATTY

And would that I could give you rest.
> (*Her hand lovingly strokes his hair.*)

JEFFERSON

You do—when I'm away you do and when I'm with you.
> (*For a moment they are silent.*)

PATTY

(*Suddenly.*)
Last night I dreamed we were back there on our mountain—at Monticello. The Tories had burnt the house. And it was under the tulip poplar—you were standing looking down at my cold face.
> (*She lifts her gaunt eyes and stares ahead of her and by the form of her beloved husband, seeing there in the future something that makes her shudder.*)

JEFFERSON

(*Gazing at her.*)
Your cold face?

PATTY

And you were weeping. I heard you say in my dream—
She was all I had—no one can ever take her place.

JEFFERSON

(*Fervently.*)
And no one can.
  (*He hugs her to him.*)

PATTY

S-sh-s-sh!
  (*Putting a finger on his lips.*)
May I be selfish with you?

JEFFERSON

(*Laughingly.*)
You couldn't be.

PATTY

When—when I die—
  (*A little sharply.*)
—don't marry again.
  (*Jefferson sits up straight and looks down at her.*)

JEFFERSON

(*Sternly.*)
What nonsense is this—this dying? Of course I'd never marry again.
  (*Laughing.*)
And your promise, sweetheart—as a dear little gray-haired widow—you must put some flowers now and then above my poor old bones.

PATTY

(*Almost vehemently.*)
You promise, you promise.
(*She flings out her arms and pulls him tightly to her bosom.*)
It's selfish, it's selfish, but so—my love.
(*She holds him to her, then after a moment she goes on murmuringly.*)
.... You remember the song we used to sing together when we first met?

JEFFERSON

Yes, yes.

PATTY

And you played it on your violin.
(*Half-singing.*)
"Now what is love, I pray thee fain."

JEFFERSON

(*Falling in with her.*)
"It is a sunshine mixed with rain."

PATTY

"It is a gentle pleasing pain."

JEFFERSON

"A flower that dies and springs again."

PATTY

"It is a No that would full fain."

JEFFERSON

"And this is love"—

Both

(*Now singing softly in unison.*)
"And this is love as I hear sayen."
(*He leans over and kisses the top of her bright head.*)

Jefferson

I thought I knew what love was then—
(*Shaking his head.*)
But I didn't. I know now—far better than the song says.

Patty

Yes.

Jefferson

All this absence and heart-ache and hunger for you through the years have made me know.

Patty

(*Murmuring.*)
Hunger and heartache. Do you know that this is the first Christmas we have had together since the war began.

Jefferson

(*Sitting up.*)
And after the war is over, we'll have every Christmas together—Every one, there at Monticello.

Patty

(*Anxiously.*)
And we will win this war, won't we, we will?

Jefferson

We will, somehow we will.
(*He leans his head over on her shoulder again, then straightens up.*)

Hah. And rest. You're the one that needs it. You should be resting in my arms.

PATTY

(*Pulling him back.*)
Last year I sat by this fire and waited and waited and you didn't come.

JEFFERSON

Edmund Pendleton and I were having it out up there at Fredericksburg—fighting the same old battle for religious freedom.
(*Almost irritatedly as he shifts his long frame in his chair.*)
Blast him. Smart, clever. He still keeps that bill from being passed.
(*Vehemently.*)
But it will be, it will be, Patty. You can't control the inner thinkings of the soul by outward laws and statutes. For a man's heart is free, is his own. And the relationship between him and his God is his own—and it must be so or he is no man. Think of it. Should my love for you be controlled and governed by laws on the books of the commonwealth?
(*He rises to his feet in his sudden turmoiling.*)

PATTY

(*Emphatically.*)
Now, now. You're not to preach.
(*She plucks at his sleeve and he sinks down again on his seat.*)

JEFFERSON

That's right. You've heard me say all this many times before.

(She lays her head over on his lap, and he sits stroking her hair.)
How many hours, my darling, driving those long roads from city to city, hamlet to hamlet, have I closed my eyes and seen you at home, heard your dear voice singing to the children, seen you as you worked about the house, looking after the sick ones, keeping the accounts, doctoring the slaves.
(Sighing.)
It's been hard on you. But before the Almighty I'll spare you hereafter.

PATTY

(Shaking her head.)
I don't want to be spared. I want to be with you—share with you—suffer with you in building this our country. The secret of a woman's love is giving—giving to her man.
(Martha comes in at the right.)

MARTHA

(Stopping and surveying them.)
Now that's sweet. It's sweet as it can be.

JEFFERSON

(A little sheepishly.)
Come in.

MARTHA

It's the first time in many a day, Tom Jefferson, you've taken time to sit down and tell your wife you love her. Would Christmas come oftener.
(Jefferson makes a motion to rise. Patty straightens up.)
Nah, nah, nah.
(Gazing at them.)

And look at her. Thin as a whippoorwill. Well praise be to God on high, in six more months you will be free of this governor's office and can take her home to Monticello.

PATTY

(*A little strongly.*)
But there will be another term.

MARTHA

(*Quickly.*)
Well, he won't be asked to serve it—and you'd better be glad.
(*Gesturing behind her.*)
Some men out there want to see you.

PATTY

Oh, please, for one night—can't they leave him in peace.

JEFFERSON

Who are they?

MARTHA

They're from the house of delegates. I told them you were engaged.

JEFFERSON

(*Rising quickly.*)
I'll have to see them.
(*Aunt Nancy comes in at the rear and she and Jefferson help Patty out. Martha turns back the way she came. Jefferson kisses his wife goodnight at the door. Several legislators come in now, pushing almost by Martha. They are shaking the touches of snow from their coats and hats.*)

First Man
(*Snappingly.*)
It's very important—I insist.

Martha
(*Protestingly.*)
Important, of course it's important. Everything is important—including a man's dying wife.
(*Jefferson re-enters the scene.*)

Jefferson
Never mind, Martha. Gentlemen.
(*Martha looks at the men, then at Jefferson and goes half-angrily out at the rear.*)

First Man
Your excellency, we will come to the point. We are a committee sent to you by the senate and the house now convened in session.

Jefferson
(*Coldly.*)
Yes.

Second Man
These militia men you have assembled here in Williamsburg—
(*He gestures toward the outdoors.*)
—we are to inquire if they are for home service.

Jefferson
No, they are not.

Third Man
(*With a look of triumph about him.*)
Hah!

First Man

We are well sent then. The house and senate require that they be kept here in Virginia.

Jefferson

(*Now speaking with sudden passion.*)
I have said to you before, gentlemen, and I repeat it—when General Washington calls for men and arms I shall send them—as long as there is one musket and one man in Virginia able to be sent. And that goes for the army in the south also.

Second Man

(*Loudly.*)
And again we protest this practice.

Voices

Aye, aye.

First Man

And the house and senate protest it.

Jefferson

Are we to trust our commander-in-chief or are we not? Are we to be true to the other colonies that are working so valiantly with us?

Third Man

(*Boldly.*)
And *I* have said it before and I say it again. Horatio Gates ought to be commander-in-chief. He conquered Burgoyne and that's the only victory we've had.
(*Vehemently.*)
The only one!

Jefferson

When I took the office of governor I made it clear to all the members of our legislature and to our people—I consider this to be the cause of all the colonies and not of one. And so does General Washington consider it.

Third Man

Washington! Tell me, when is he to win a victory, I ask you?

Voices

(*Again.*)
Aye, aye.

Jefferson

As long as he is able to keep his army in the field—that is a victory. And he has stood like a bulwark, has shown himself a great and capable leader.
(*Raising his hands, half-clenched.*)
You have known him personally. So have I. And as it was said of a man nearly two thousand years ago, I find no fault in him.
(*Taking up a letter from the desk and reading from it in flowing earnest words.*)
"If you value the cause for which we fight, send me more men. Send me arms, supplies. My forces are weakened so fearfully it would be fatal to us for the enemy to learn the truth."
(*Taking a second letter from the desk and reading likewise.*)
"We must have another levy of at least one thousand militia by autumn. We must."
(*Dropping the letter on the table again.*)
And we are sending him a pitiful half-armed three hundred. Gentlemen, I am not a military authority, but—

Voices

(*Breaking in discordantly.*)
No, no. That's right. You are not.

Jefferson

(*Blazing out at them.*)
Nor are you. But it is good reason that as long as we can keep our armies in the field—one in the north, one in the south—undefeated, our cause is not entirely lost.

First Man

(*Now beginning to match fiery words with Jefferson.*)
And I tell you, sir, that you have weakened our native state until she lies helpless for the trampling feet of any invader. And the Tories along the Eastern Shore and the Tidewater are rising and arming themselves in bands.

Jefferson

And I am taking steps immediately against these Tories.

Third Man

Aye, another proclamation, no doubt.

Jefferson

That too perhaps. And so, gentlemen—
(*He waves his hand as if dismissing them.*)
—by virtue of the powers vested in me as head of this commonwealth I shall continue to comply in so far as I am able with the demands of our military leaders. Good day.
(*But the members stand their ground.*)

First Man

We want you to know, sir, we feel you are wrong.

Fourth Man

My people in the western hills are calling for help against the Indians—
  (*Bitterly.*)
—our former allies that have now turned against us in our weakness. The poor women and children in the valleys are being murdered.
  (*Angrily.*)
And why? Because our soldiers have all been sent to General Washington or cut to pieces and lost in the swamps of the Carolinas.

Jefferson

I know—aye—that is a heartbreaking thing. But Colonel Clark is raising a levy in the west to march against these Indians.

Fourth Man

Aye, he will levy on rocks and hills and trees. There are no men left.

Jefferson

George Clark will find men.
  (*Fiercely, half to himself.*)
He must—he will.

First Man

And that is your final word?

Jefferson

  (*Impatiently.*)
It is.

Second Man

And if invasion comes?

Jefferson

(*Wearily.*)
Then it must come.

First Man

And you know that if Virginia is conquered, then the colonies are cut in two from the mountains to the sea and our cause is lost forever.
(*They all stare accusingly at Jefferson. He lowers his glance and gazes at the floor in thought.*)

Third Man

Our beloved commonwealth is already left like an empty bag—empty, you hear me, gentlemen!

Voices

Aye, aye.

Jefferson

(*Still staring ahead of him.*)
I have heard you can catch things in an empty bag.
(*They gaze at him inquiringly, as his words run on a little abstractedly and monologue-like.*)
If the invader comes into our commonwealth mayhap the two armies we have struggled to keep alive can turn upon him, one from the north and one from the south. And if in God's good grace the French fleet could arrive on the eastern coast at that time, then—then—
(*He snaps his fingers in the air.*)

First Man

(*Completely outdone.*)
Are you ill, sir?
(*Chuckling grimly.*)
Never before have I heard that the way to conquer your enemy is first to let him conquer you.

Second Man

And where is this French fleet? Has anyone seen it?

Third Man

(*Bitterly.*)
Oh yes, France will sign a treaty—on paper. But it's still on paper.

Jefferson

(*Coldly.*)
You forget brave Lafayette is now with General Washington.

Third Man

A stripling boy out for adventure.

Second Man

We know the policy of the French all right—they wear out one enemy against the other while they sit and wait, wait, saving their own strength.
(*Flinging up a clenched fist.*)
It's true, gentlemen.

Voices

Aye.

Fourth Man

And when we are bled to death in our weakness then she will sweep in and retake Detroit, Vincennes and the Northwest Territory.

Jefferson

(*Angrily.*)
That is a shameful travesty upon a brave ally—and upon our great statesman Benjamin Franklin.

First Man

Come, gentlemen, we must make our report to the assembly.

Second Man

(*Somewhat maliciously.*)
And we demand that you rescind your decision—to send the last of our militia to Washington.

Jefferson

The decision must stand.

Second Man

Then we may adopt sterner measures.

First Man

(*Coldly.*)
We may demand your resignation.

Jefferson

(*Almost vehemently.*)
You shall not have it if you do.

First Man

(*Boldly.*)
So—you may find yourself an object of impeachment, sir.
(*His voice is loud and angry. Jefferson looks around at him shocked by the words. He sinks down in the chair—a little hopelessly.*)

JEFFERSON

And it was less than a year ago you same gentlemen came to Monticello—pleading with me to become your governor and leader—and now—
>   (*He throws out his hands in an ironic gesture. The men gaze at him another instant, then turn and go out the way they came. Jefferson moves abstractedly toward his desk and papers. The door opens and Patty Jefferson comes in almost distrait. She is barefooted and dressed in her nightgown. Jefferson hurries to her. His very devotion makes him almost irritable with her.*)

In mercy's name! You must sleep, Patty.
>   (*Calling.*)

Aunt Nancy!

PATTY

>   (*As she goes up to him.*)

How can I sleep!
>   (*Gazing at him with anguished love and pain.*)

I heard what they said to you, those men. Oh, my darling, they are killing you.

JEFFERSON

>   (*Roughly.*)

They are not.

PATTY

You pace the floor at night. You never rest—never.
>   (*Sobbingly.*)

And they are killing you.
>   (*She clings tightly to him.*)

But you won't resign, will you? You won't let them beat you down?

Jefferson

Certainly I shan't resign.
(*Trying to comfort her.*)
With you to stand by me I'll outface them all.
(*Old Aunt Nancy comes hurriedly in. She carries a shawl in her hand.*)

Aunt Nancy

Well he'p my life—Miss Patty—this time I could whup you!—and you—all bare-footed.
(*Wrapping the shawl around Patty's shoulders and then speaking to Jefferson.*)
Yessuh—resign—dat's what you ought to do, Massa Tom. And go back to Monticello.

Jefferson

Get her to bed at once.

Aunt Nancy

Come on, baby lamb—I tek care of you—

Patty

(*Her words beginning to run a little wild.*)
They can't beat us down—they can't—together we stand—
(*Her voice soaring into an almost hysterical cry.*)
—stand together to the end, fighting on—until we win—until we win!
(*She sags suddenly and weakly down. Jefferson catches her, and holds her to him with a groan. He lifts her in his arms and takes her back to her bed through the door at the rear, Aunt Nancy following. The light dims out on the scene and comes up on the left front of the center stage. Hugh Taylor and*

Cephus Sicklemore appear there. They are footsore and weary and their clothes and shoes in wretched condition. Cephus has an old stuffed budget on his back and carries an ancient battered musket. Hugh has a sort of weather-worn roll strapped diagonally across his shoulder and is unarmed save for a cudgel or walking stick. Cephus gazes about him and sniffs the air.)

Cephus

Ah, Lord ha' mercy on my soul—is it a dream, Captain Taylor, and you and me walking the streets of the New Jerusalem—or is this Williamsburg?

Hugh

Williamsburg, Cephus.

Cephus

Lord, and I never expected it. There at Valley Forge with all them shells bursting around me, I said—I give up my final hope forevermore.

Hugh

There was nothing but snow and ice at Valley Forge, Cephus.

Cephus

Then 'twas the trees popping loud like cannon under their weight and calamity of sleet.
    (*Looking off and shaking his shoulders like a dog.*)
Dad jog it, I wonder do my light, my honey-love, still prove faithful unto me? Ah, Mammy Huzzitt, I kiss your lily white hand.

THE COMMON GLORY 175

Hugh

You have but time to see her, and we must be on our way.

Cephus

This time, Captain Taylor, I'm a marrying man, made manifest and sanctified down to the ground.

Hugh

Hurry along with ye whilst I speak to the governor.

Cephus

Eck! His honor the governor? Then let my two eyes both behold him together at once, and so pay my deep respects unto him.
 (*Hugh and Cephus move over toward the side stage at the left. The light comes up on the scene again as before, and dies out behind them. Jefferson has returned into the room and is now pacing up and down in thought. Hugh comes up farther into the light. Jefferson stops his pacing, blinks out at him, then moves forward with outstretched hands. Hugh steps into the room.*)

Jefferson

Hugh, my lad!
 (*He shakes his hand fervently with both of his.*)

Hugh

 (*Saluting.*)
Your excellency.

Cephus

 (*Crowding forward and calling out.*)
Long live your worship!
 (*He pulls off his old hat.*)

JEFFERSON

I scarcely knew ye, Cephus. You have changed... Greetings.

CEPHUS

(*His face swept with sudden mournfulness.*)
Aye, that I have changed. I am but a walking skellitun now, your reverence, and all the easeful fat that once was me they have marched and sweated it away in the cause of freedom.
(*Sighing.*)
Ah, soul! And the drops of my lard have greased half the highways of this continent.

JEFFERSON

You have suffered, Cephus.

CEPHUS

Aye.
(*Giving his hat a twirl.*)
But long live liberty, still say I.
(*Slapping his musket.*)
As the Good Book says, Saul slew his thousands, David his tens of thousands—
(*With a sudden laugh.*)
But then the deadfall of modesty drops on my tongue, your worship—heh-heh-heh—and I say no more.

JEFFERSON

Virginia is proud of you, Cephus.

CEPHUS

Ah, and if only she would honor me with a little teeny-einsy piece of gold.

THE COMMON GLORY

(He holds up his hand and pinches the air between his thumb and forefinger.)

JEFFERSON

(With a laugh.)
There is hardly a piece of gold in all this commonwealth.

CEPHUS

(Unmollified and doubting.)
Ahm.

HUGH

Away now, Cephus. I'll join ye.

CEPHUS

(Saluting and backing away.)
Aye, aye, sir.
   (He goes off into the shadow the way he came, suddenly bursting into a cheerful stave of song.)

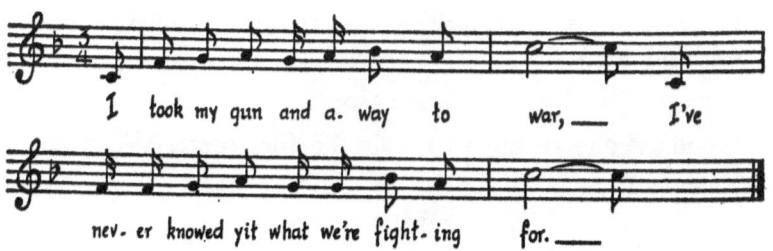

JEFFERSON

(To Hugh.)
Sit down, man.
   (Hugh sinks down into a chair.)
And General Washington—When did you last see him?

Hugh

Three weeks ago.

Jefferson

His health?

Hugh

He still stays on his feet.

Jefferson

(*Clinching his fist.*)
Aye, and he will to the last! And you?

Hugh

I'm invalided home for guard duty till I recover.
(*Jefferson looks his sympathy.*)

Jefferson

You'd best report to General Thomas Nelson.

Hugh

I have. I'm assigned over to the garrison at Jamestown—with my men.

Jefferson

Good. We're trying to repair the fort there. We need your help.

Hugh

(*Wearily.*)
I'm afraid I won't be much help anywhere for sometime.

Jefferson

Your advice and experience will be invaluable.
(*Hugh hesitates, then turns to Jefferson.*)

Hugh

And Mistress Eileen—how is she?

Jefferson

Well, I presume.

Hugh

Thank God.

Jefferson

She is at the plantation with her father. I regret that fact.
    (*Hugh looks his query. Jefferson pauses a moment, then continues.*)
I am having to take desperate measures, Hugh. An evil force in Virginia has been actively at work of recent months, under cover, under ground—spreading rumors of defeat, causing dissension among the people, among the troops even. Food stores have been burned, laden boats scuttled in the river, as if a corps of invisible night riders were at work. And spies are even in our council chambers. One man has brought this about—Robert Gordon.
    (*Hugh looks at him, saying nothing.*)
His power must be destroyed.

Hugh

And Eileen?

Jefferson

Must bear the consequences.

Hugh

Have you proof?

Jefferson

Yes—a captured message from Gordon to Cornwallis in the south. I have arranged for a picked body of men under Colonel Davies tonight to surround his house and take him prisoner—alive or dead.

Hugh

(*Spontaneously.*)
But she would be in danger!—
   (*Jefferson stares at him. He bows his head a little lamely.*)
I'm sorry, sir.

Jefferson

It must be done, Hugh.

Hugh

(*Raising his head.*)
Then allow me to go with the party. She will need me. I might protect her.
   (*With a wan smile.*)
I once said there'd come a time when she'd need me.
   (*Holding out his hands.*)
And now these two hands are weak things to offer her. May I go?

Jefferson

(*After a moment.*)
As you will.

Hugh

My thanks, sir.
   (*He rises, but staggers a bit. Jefferson puts out his hand. Hugh nods his appreciation, turns and goes back into the shadow the way he came. Jefferson stares after him, then in anguish grips his hair with his hands, his elbows touching each other in front of him and turns about the room. Sitting down at his desk he begins tackling his correspondence doggedly.*)

The light fades down on the scene and comes up on the narrator.)

NARRATOR

That night the daring Colonel Davies with his men surrounded the home of the great planter and loyalist and took him prisoner. Some of the Tory guards defending the place were killed and Gordon was forced to yield. But at the last moment he set fire with his own hand to his great mansion—which with all his priceless books and hangings and works of art was consumed to the ground. And back in Williamsburg he faced Jefferson defiant and unafraid.

(The light fades out from the narrator and comes up on the right front center stage.)

SCENE 3

A committee room in the capitol, with the usual wainscoted and plastered walls, and paneled mantelpiece. Two large windows at the rear give a view of the trees and a few houses of Williamsburg in the distance. Jefferson is pacing the floor. Robert Gordon is standing cold and implacable in the center of the room. In the rear by the door are two patriot soldiers with bayoneted muskets. Over to one side Eileen is sitting bent in a chair, her face stained with weeping. Hugh stands behind her. For a moment the scene is silent as Jefferson paces back and forth. Finally he stops and turns to Gordon.

JEFFERSON

I am not an unreasonable man, Cousin Robert. We will compromise. Give me your pledge to remain neutral—and you may go free.

GORDON

That is a pledge I cannot give.
 (*Jefferson's temper almost gets the better of him.*)

JEFFERSON

Not even that!
 (*With a great effort of will he controls his anger and frustration. As he paces.*)
You're an obstinate man, Cousin Robert.

GORDON

So are we both. Our Randolph inheritance perchance.

JEFFERSON

(*Turning on him again.*)
Blind and obstinate.
(*Intensely.*)
There in the house of burgesses day after day, year after year you saw it—saw how oppression and injustice were being prepared against us, saw how we one by one rose up to fight for our rights against enslaving tyranny.

GORDON

So ye called it in *your* blindness. And day after day, year after year you saw how I counseled patience—yes, against this madness, I pleaded your duty, our duty, to the throne and to England.
(*Raging.*)
But no, it must be liberty, liberty. Like spoiled and perverse children you needs must throw off all restraint. Well, now you see the poisonous fruits of your wild policy.

JEFFERSON

(*Almost shrilly.*)
And you still refuse your pledge of neutrality.

GORDON

(*Sneeringly.*)
These years I have suffered in silence, bided my time, waited until the tide of power turned in the king's favor. And now it has turned. And when my friend Cornwallis arrives from the Carolinas and the British fleet arrives from the north, thousands of loyal citizens from the mountains to the sea will be ready to leap to arms and take this beloved Dominion back for the king. And then

the nightmare of fire that you and others have lighted shall be quenched forever in your guilty blood.

JEFFERSON

You are mad if you think there will be such a rising.

GORDON

Time has already proved who is mad.
  (*Wagging his head.*)
And I will not forget. I will not forget the sudden and midnight raid upon my peace and quiet—the insult to me and my daughter—
  (*Suddenly pointing at Hugh.*)
—this workman—leading cutthroats and highwaymen against me.
  (*Eileen makes a movement as if to defend Hugh against her father's charge, then is still.*)
Your cause is lost, Thomas Jefferson, and you know it.

JEFFERSON

  (*His nerves on edge, yelling.*)
Once more—will you pledge your word!

GORDON

  (*With cold serenity.*)
You're a good actor—nigh as good as the loud-mouth Patrick Henry. And so here we meet, as in a play.
  (*Musingly.*)
And I remember the times you were our guest, the music we played, the science and art and books and philosophy we talked, and here we meet—bitter enemies.
  (*Shaking his head.*)
See now the woe you have wrought—this civil war—

father aligned against son, brother against brother—family against family.
(*With a cry.*)
But the right will prevail.

JEFFERSON

(*Loudly.*)
Aye, our right, and we'll make it prevail.

GORDON

There is only one right—that America and England should remain one united nation. It is a mad and eternal wrong to break them apart. Whatever evils have arisen, might have been settled, they will be settled. Even as William Pitt said, a mighty and glorious England in this world is the guarantee of strength and light to that world. And you fools from the beginning have determined to break the empire in two. And as she is broken, so is man everywhere weakened and broken. But now the hour of victory draws nigh, and it will be whole again.
(*He gazes at Jefferson, triumphant.*)

JEFFERSON

(*Looking at him coldly, implacably.*)
This day the commonwealth of Virginia confiscates your property—your lands, your possessions, Robert Gordon.

GORDON

(*As coldly.*)
You confiscate the ruins left by fire.

JEFFERSON

(*In horror.*)
What!

Gordon

The trouble with you, Jefferson, is you don't believe in God and the anointed of God. I do. And so what is required in their service I give and will—even unto death. I have burnt my mansion and all that's in it.
> (*For a moment Jefferson stares at him. In his mind is all the tragic picture of the loss of the things he himself admires and cherishes. Rage shakes his gaunt form.*)

Jefferson

Then see if this god you believe in—this pitiful paunchy being that wears a crown and befouls the throne of England can help you now! ... The guard!
> (*The two soldiers step inside the door. Eileen springs up in alarm and even Gordon glances around somewhat startled. Jefferson snarls out his command.*)

Take this Tory away. Confine him in irons in the common gaol till he be tried. And if found guilty——
> (*Jefferson's eyes are now cold and cruel as he gazes at Gordon. His words have been spat into the air. Eileen rushes to her father.*)

Eileen

Father!
> (*One of the guards starts to jerk Eileen loose from her father, but Hugh steps quickly up and stops him. Eileen stares speechlessly at Jefferson. Gordon blinks a little as if unbelievingly and then straightens up.*)

Gordon

I warn you, Jefferson, make no mistake—if harm comes to me or my daughter, your life shall answer for it.

JEFFERSON

(*Sharply.*)
Eileen shall receive the protection of my family.
(*Striking the table with his fist.*)
Come, we will take him away.

EILEEN

(*Moving swiftly in front of Jefferson.*)
Please, Cousin Jefferson. Please.
(*She seizes his arm fiercely.*)
You see I'm not proud. I beg for him—for my father. On my knees I——

GORDON

(*Loudly.*)
Eileen!
(*Scathingly.*)
Would my·daughter so demean herself as to beg my safety of this—traitor!
(*Jefferson pushes Eileen firmly away from him. Gordon starts forward. The soldiers take hold of his arms, but he flings them off. Jefferson goes out at the rear, and Gordon gives Eileen a hard proud look, then turns and marches out after him. Eileen sinks down into a chair, sobbing. Hugh stands beside her.*)

EILEEN

The shame, the shame! It will kill him. It will, Hugh.
(*She springs up as if to go out of the scene. Hugh steps between her and the door. She sinks down into the chair again.*)

HUGH

There's nothing you can do now. Later you can see him.
(*He gazes at her with tired bloodshot eyes. She sits*

a moment with bent head, her shoulders shaking in struggling sobs. Her name comes through Hugh's lips intense and low and yearning.)

Eileen.

Eileen

(*Twisting her hands together, her voice a cry.*)
What have they done to him!—Oh, my father!

Hugh

(*His gaze burning at her.*)
It had to be this way—blood against blood. And so it will keep on being till we win.

Eileen

Hah. You win!
  (*Going on defiantly.*)
But father will never yield. Never.

Hugh

Nor will Mr. Jefferson. Come, I'll take you to Mistress Martha.

Eileen

(*A little shrilly.*)
And I'm glad, glad my father will not.
  (*Straightening up as if ashamed of her weakness.*)
He is great and strong and good. He is a man. His pride and honor are his life.

Hugh

(*With a touch of bitter sarcasm.*)
And nobody else in the world is strong and good. The rest are weaklings.

Eileen

Yes. Yes.

(*Looking up at him.*)

And I hate all who fight against him, who make him suffer.

Hugh

Then, tonight you hate me too.

(*She turns away her head. He goes on bitterly.*)

Pride and honor—all right. So do I have my pride and honor as a man too.

(*He suddenly takes one of her hands and holds it tightly to him.*)

That's why I fight this war—and thousands of other poor devils like me—that we can be men, free men. Your father is my enemy, and I will stand against him till the end for what I believe—

(*She tries to wrench her hand free as he goes on.*)

—even as he stands against me. But you, you are not my enemy. You are everything but that. You are— Oh, Eileen—

(*His words tumbling out.*)

How long it's been, I don't remember the years, there on the plantation when I used to do your bidding—

(*Almost abruptly.*)

I love you, Eileen.

(*She makes a movement in her chair, then sits still and straight.*)

I used to wake up in the morning—and the day was empty, the sun didn't rise, until I saw you there in the garden or somewhere about the place. And there in the hills to the west I saw only your face. I could never forget you.

(He looks down at her, a wan hard smile playing about his tense lips.)
I tell you now—I love you. And I want to help you.

EILEEN

(After a moment.)
Then you will. You must help me.
   (She looks up and stares searchingly into his face.)

HUGH

And I fight this war for you too, Eileen—for the life that we could have together—here in the new America we'll work to build.

EILEEN

Cousin Jefferson might listen to you.
   (Excitedly.)
Together we could go to General Washington himself—plead father's case to him. He would listen.

HUGH

(Harshly as he drops her hand.)
So you ask me to betray my cause.

EILEEN

If—if you love me—as you say.

HUGH

Then you would hate me indeed.

EILEEN

(Passionately.)
No, Hugh, no.

Hugh

(*Roughly.*)

Look at me—straight—tell me. If I did this for you—then I might hope for—

(*He hesitates, then speaks the words shortly and simply.*)

—hope for your love.

(*A moment they look at each other. Her eyes waver. Hugh goes on with irritable triumph.*)

See, you can't deny it. I'd be a weakling and deserve the scorn you'd give a weakling.

(*He stands in front of her. She rises, then turns. And now a hard wan smile plays about her lips also.*)

Eileen

You are strong and stubborn too, Hugh.

Hugh

Like your father then.

Eileen

(*In a low voice.*)

Yes.

Hugh

For that I thank you.

(*For a moment they gaze at each other, man and woman, each with a deep and turmoiling suffering and perplexity, finding in that suffering and perplexity for an instant an identity of being.*)

Eileen

(*Her lips suddenly trembling, as her eyes search his haggard face.*)

And ah, what you have suffered in this war!
(*She puts out her hand as if to touch his arm, then lets it drop.*)

Hugh

(*Fervently.*)
Eileen.
(*She turns and goes out at the rear. A moment he stands still, then follows after her. The scene blacks out and the light comes up again on the narrator.*)

Narrator

The arrest and imprisonment of Gordon halted the Tory risings for awhile, but it seemed now as if the affairs of the commonwealth were past mending. The people had given of their last crust, farms had been completely stripped of their cattle and their work stock. And neither men, arms nor supplies were longer to be found. Insatiable war had devoured them.

But Jefferson was still tireless in his efforts—writing late at night his endless letters to his leaders and lieutenants throughout the Dominion. And from dawn to dark many a day his fever-wracked body was in the saddle as he rode from post to post to talk with the men and encourage them. And like the fading of his own hopes was the wasting away of his young idolized wife.

Now the danger of invasion grew real, and rumors flew thick and fast. The weak garrisons guarding the strategic points along the rivers and harbors were swept with hysteria, among them the old fort at Jamestown where Hugh Taylor and his pitiful forces were on guard.
(*The light fades from the narrator and comes up on the center stage.*)

SCENE 4

The ruined churchyard at Jamestown. In the right foreground is the old crumbled and ivy-covered tower, and in the shadowy background here and there the muffled forms of bushes and a few trees. Standing on a drum of wood against the tower is Hugh Taylor. His sword is drawn, his face pale, and he is pleading with the hysterical, angry and turmoiling small garrison below and around him not to desert the fort. The garrison consists of some fifteen or twenty men—a few of them still in American uniforms and the rest of them in nondescript garments of all kinds. Several of them are unarmed. A few have swords at their waists, others carry tomahawks, clubs or cudgels.

Hugh
(Shouting.)
Back, I tell you—back to your posts!

Voices
(In a swirl of snarling mockery.)
Feed us!

Other Voices
Give us clothes!

Still Other Voices
We are starving!

(The rebellious men are led by our friend Sergeant Jack. Cephus is skittishly teetering around in the scene dragging his old musket with him. He wants to help his captain but can do nothing.)

Hugh

If you desert this fort—you may be shot.

Sergeant Jack

(*Stepping forward.*)
Many's the night we have wanted to be shot—standing here starving and freezing to the bone! Are you with me, men!

Voices

(*Calling out.*)
Leave! Let us leave now!

Other Voices

Home! We'll go home!

All

(*In a great longing cry.*)
Home!
(*With the last of his strength, Hugh springs out before them with his drawn sword.*)

Hugh

I'll kill the first man that—
(*But Sergeant Jack and two or three other men whirl upon him, tear his sword from his hand and send him plunging and staggering back against the old tower. He falls up against it and clutches the doorway for support. Cephus would run at Sergeant Jack in defense of Hugh, but Jack brings Hugh's sword down through the air at him with a great swish. The valiant soldier falls back before the blood-thirsty blade with a "whiff" of terror and disappears behind the tower.*)

Cephus

(With a wild cry as he disappears.)
Ee-yah!

Sergeant Jack

(Throwing the sword at Hugh's feet.)
We're sorry, sir. You have been a good captain. But we can no longer serve you. And now for us the war is ended.

Men

(With a high cheering cry.)
'Ray! 'Ray!
(They start out. At this moment Jefferson comes hurrying in from the right front.)

Hugh

(With a gasping cry.)
Governor Jefferson! Thank God you have come.
(As if the strength goes out of him he yields the battle over to Jefferson. He slides down onto an old log seat at the base of the tower.)

Voices

(Muttering, as they turn around.)
The governor! It's the governor.
(Sergeant Jack and the men draw back a step or two before Jefferson's stern figure. Jefferson gazes out at them. He sees the men's piteous condition, the exposure and suffering showing in their forms and faces, the hurt spectacle of pain. The hardness of his manner softens instinctively and the soldiers instantly sense it. Their attitude hardens.)

Jefferson

(*Holding his voice calm.*)
You men have sworn an oath to defend your native Virginia. I warn you—if you break that oath—

Sergeant Jack

(*Coldly and in the same quiet manner as Jefferson now.*)
Virginia long ago has broken her oath with us, sir.

Jefferson

She has not. We are doing all we can for you.

Sergeant Jack

And every day here we die—this morning two men, yesterday three, the day before that two. We had no blankets even to bury them in. Naked we put them in the ground out there—our comrades—naked as they came into the world. Well their mothers could not see their pitiful shrunken forms.
(*Slapping himself.*)
This rag I call a coat belonged to one of them.

Jefferson

So have we all suffered. And we must continue to suffer to the end—to the end, I tell you.

Sergeant Jack

And this is the end. We bespoke a boat coming up the river. The British have landed at Portsmouth.

Jefferson

It is only a rumor. It must be proved.

Sergeant Jack

And are we to sit here helpless—to be taken prisoner and crammed in a stinking prison ship to die! No.

Voices

(*Yelling.*)
No, no!

Sergeant Jack

It's you, sir, that have robbed Virginia of her strength—left us here weak and helpless. And now you order us back to duty. Well, sir, we will not go. Our duty now is to ourselves—to our loved ones who need us.

Other Voices

(*In fury, emboldened by the sergeant.*)
Down with the governor!

Still Other Voices

Down with Jefferson!
(*Jefferson stands defiant in front of them, his long arms outspread in one more effort to stop the surge that has begun in them.*)

Jefferson

I plead with you, men, I beg you as men—to stand firm at this hour—to—

Sergeant Jack

(*Shouting.*)
Come on, men! Away!
(*They sweep over Jefferson, and with Sergeant Jack at their head, trample pell-mell away into the darkness at the right front. Jefferson stands helpless and bereft in the scene. A moment he stands so. A great*

sigh goes out of him. He feels his way through the air over to the old tower and sinks down on the drum of wood. His voice rises again, monologic and anguished.)

JEFFERSON

That it should happen here—this cowardice, this betrayal of our cause—here, here at this sacred spot.

HUGH

(*Mirthlessly as he sits hunched over.*)
Me and my men have not found it sacred.

JEFFERSON

Here was the birthplace of our nation, Hugh. Here where we sit tonight—a hundred and seventy-five years ago it all began here.

HUGH

And here it ends.

JEFFERSON

(*Loudly.*)
No!

HUGH

The nation that was to be.

JEFFERSON

And yet shall be!

HUGH

Our cause is lost, Mr. Jefferson.

JEFFERSON

(*Vehemently.*)
No, it is not lost!

Hugh

I will rest on my bed now.

> (*He turns and crawls into the doorway of the old church tower to his pallet of straw.*)

Here's where I sleep—what time I do sleep.

> (*Jefferson sits a lonely tragic figure there against the old church tower, the light a little brighter on him in emphasis. In the gloom at the rear and surrounding scene the gray slash of a flat tombstone or two can be clearly discerned now. Hugh's words come out again, running lightly, feverishly from within the tower.*)

I have read your writings, sir—and Thomas Paine's. And I followed you into this war, believing in you—the way thousands of others did—in freedom, justice, self-government for men. That was to be the common glory of us all—as you put it in your speeches. True, it is common enough—sir—

> (*Bitterly.*)

—and there is no glory in it.

Jefferson

God forgive you, Hugh Taylor.

Hugh

Aye. But a man has to believe the truth of his own eyes. If you are right, why don't people see it. Ah, the people! The great and noble people. Where are they? Throughout the land—worse than before—men swapping and buying and trading in the life blood of us poor fools who have gone forth to die on the battlefield. These ragged shoes I wear—they cost ten times their worth! A morsel of bread and meat require a king's ransom. And congress—wrangling in debates, unable to act. And so hour by hour, day by day our cause has perished, and we with it.

JEFFERSON

You are ill, Hugh, weak with fever now. Later you will have your faith again—you will still fight for it—and for your love.

HUGH

Ah—

JEFFERSON

Eileen loves you, Hugh.
>   (*Hugh is silent as he lays himself down on his pallet. The light fades down on him. Jefferson continues his monologue.*)

We must keep fighting. Here in this hallowed spot was likewise a struggle, a harder struggle even—down to starvation. We have not starved yet. Are we less men than they were, these pioneers, these mothers and daughters, these little children—the multitudes that perished here?
>   (*Crying out into the night.*)

Are we?

HUGH

(*Still lightly from the shadow.*)
Lying here one night I dreamed a dream, your excellency—
>   (*Ironically.*)

—about this hallowed spot—a voice speaking, speaking out of this tower above me there—saying, a curse is upon us all and upon this place—this place of evil.

JEFFERSON

A curse? Evil?

HUGH

Here were the helpless and innocent murdered—the pitiful Indians robbed of their land. And the first whimpering black Africans were dragged here in chains and sold as human flesh under the slaver's whip. Here slavery began—upon this very spot. So—your pioneers!

JEFFERSON

Aye, these were evil things.
> (*He bows his head over as if in exhaustion. Then his voice rises again in its pleading monologue.*)

A curse for cruelty and sin, that would be just. But, but—
> (*He shakes his shoulders in weariness and pain. Still the fighting spirit in him will not die. He must push his way on through somehow.*)

But beyond the cruelty and the sin, Hugh, beyond the killing and the enslavement of the innocent there was a light, an idea. It started here. Like a spark at first, a faint ember—then growing, blown into strength by the dying breath of those who served it. Down the years it grew—and now it is a torch, a torch which we carry in our hand—the torch of freedom. And shall we let it fall from our grasp?
> (*Crying out.*)

Never!
> (*He staggers to his feet as if to charge some enemy that stands in hindrance of his way, but weakly sinks down again.*)

But ah, we have no help. Our strength is gone, our men departed. Where are our men!
> (*Gazing about him.*)

Even your loyal Cephus has deserted us.
> (*He bends his head over again, hugging his knees, a nausea of fever and frustration in him.*)

I too have wondered, Hugh, about evil and sin. This war has uprooted families, destroyed homes, torn loved ones

asunder, brought forth murder and rapine and pillage and the muck and filth and horror of destruction. Is that the way the truth must come, the truth for which we live?
  (*Groggily.*)
In Williamsburg jail tonight Robert Gordon lies sick, emaciated and perchance dying. And I put him there! And this struggle is killing my heart's life, the wife I love. Resign, quit, give up, says my sister. Sue for peace, patch up a peace—the king will forgive. All will be well. Fool, fool, she calls me.
  (*He beats his fists against his knees.*)
But I won't, Hugh. I won't. I can't.
  (*He rises and moves waveringly about the scene, the terrific search and inquiry continuing within him.*)
When the cause is right, it must live, men must make it live. Through death and destruction—it must live.
  (*His voice ringing out in the night as he seems to glimpse something of the truth for which he searches.*)
That's it, Hugh, that's it. Out of death and destruction to make life. It is easy to make a good thing out of a good thing. But good out of evil—that's the challenge. Yes, out of the cruelty and sin and even enslavement here—to use them, to help build the republic in which they shall not be—shall not be because they have been here!
  (*He stands a moment with lifted face, swaying as if about to fall. He strikes his breast with his clenched fist.*)
With my lips I say these words. But where is their meaning? They are cold, dead. Lonely. Lonely, and in here—death, death.

Hugh

  (*Muttering from the darkness.*)
Hah, so.

JEFFERSON

(*Gesturing toward him.*)

Sleep, sleep like the dead—sleep. If only we all could sleep. Aye, as it says in the play—after life's fitful fever—
(*He feels his way to his seat, sinks down and stretches himself out weakly back against the old tower. The light dims down on him somewhat as he slowly falls into a black sleep of emptiness and despair. From the darkness a low humming sets up in the chorus and continues, moving outward in sympathy and condoling harmony over the scene.*)

Narrator's Voice

(From the darkness as the chorus continues humming.)

There in that old churchyard on that winter night Jefferson wrestled to see beyond the abyss of failure to the day of hope, to the truth that lives beyond error and pain. He wrestled against the enemy that always waits in ruined places to pull men down when they weaken—the temptation of death—even as you and I—when we have felt the urge to yield up the battle, to give over to the figure with the enfolding dark wings whereunder there is no remembrance, no grief, nor struggle any more. And like Jacob of old on his pillow of stones he dreamed a dream.

(There is a sudden rumble of sound as if underground, then a flash of lightning, breaking in the graveyard at the rear. The chorus stops. A funereal and ghostly green light brightens in the shadow at the right of the old tower. Standing there as if risen out of one of the flat-slabbed graves is the figure of Death, a tall dark woman dressed in a flowing black robe and with her cascade of rich hair black as midnight tumbling behind her shoulders down to her waist. Her eyes are large and bright, her face avid and desirous and under its thin covering of mouldy flesh bears a skeletal shape and outline resembling Patty Jefferson. The figure comes toward Jefferson, and we see the sleeper suddenly grasp his head with his hands as if feeling an hallucination within his brain. The ensuing bits of dialogue between Death and Jefferson in the dream are spoken in the voice of the narrator.)

JEFFERSON

(*Huskily, through the narrator.*)
Who is that?

DEATH

(*Mellifluously, through the narrator.*)
I'm death, I live here.

JEFFERSON

(*Through the narrator as before, sighing.*)
Gentle death.
 (*The figure comes over toward him.*)

DEATH

(*Through the narrator as before.*)
I am the end you have been seeking. This is the victory—for the tired struggler, for the weary wayfarer.

JEFFERSON

(*As before, but with an inner will-power stirring in him.*)
No, not death.
 (*Gasping.*)
Life, life!

DEATH

(*As before.*)
The battle over, the endeavor done.
 (*Death now stands behind Jefferson, her great mantle lifted in two huge black wings as if ready to shroud themselves suffocatingly over the sleeper.*)

Jefferson

(As before, his head lolling.)
Life that fights on.

Death

(As before, but more seductively, lulling.)
Peace, peace.
> *(But Jefferson as if making an effort like a drowning man to beat off the suffocating influence and the slowly descending mantle calls out from the depths of his soul.)*

Jefferson

(As before, somewhat wildly.)
Let not our cause perish! Help us—Almighty God!
> *(He raises himself to a half-sitting position. The motion of the mantle is stayed. The narrator speaks in his own voice.)*

Narrator

(From the darkness.)
And as Jefferson in his dream prayed for help—so did help come to him—out of the void of the past it came, out of the depths of his need and his yearning—figures whom he had brooded and thought upon when as a student at William and Mary he had so often come to visit this shrine of a nation's birth. There we see them—the enemies of death now coming to strengthen his failing will—tokens and symbols of endurance—bright immortal witnesses to life.
> *(A low humming begins in the chorus, joined later by a soft but high and shimmering harmony of the organ in the treble clef, a shimmering like bright luminous wings beating in the air. A pulse-beat is*

sounded in the organ. Out from behind the tower comes the doughty figure of Captain John Smith in full armor. The organ plays him into the scene.)

(He steps between Death and Jefferson, as Death moves forward again, for the sleeper has sagged down into black sleep once more. The narrator continues.)

That valiant warrior—who never took defeat, who never failed—though others might fail—the father of the first colony at Jamestown—Captain John Smith.

(A little surge in the organ music makes another announcement and softens down. A second figure comes out from behind the tower at the right and steps between Death and Jefferson.)

And John Rolfe, the devout and consecrated man who gave his life that the colony might survive.

(Again the surge of music in the organ in announcement. From the right rear another figure appears. A young handsome man in late 17th century dress with a sword. He also stands protectingly near Jefferson and keeps the figure of Death back.)

And daring Nathaniel Bacon who led the first rebellion in the new world that freedom might be born here and who perished in the struggle.

(Death starts to swoop down at the sleeper still once more with her outstretched ravenous cloak. The

organ as if taking alarm again cries out suddenly with a little higher and more shimmering leap of sound. The movement of Death's cloak is again arrested. At this same instant, a pallid shine and radiance comes welling up in the interior and around the base of the old tower—beautiful as the most intense moonlight, and more unearthly as it mixes in with the green glow outside. Standing illuminated in the arched doorway of the old tower is the figure of an Indian maid with a baby in her arms, a chaplet of wild flowers in her hair, beautiful as an angel in the light. Succeeding the organ's surge, the chorus has sounded a loud harmonious chord of its own announcement, sinking down to a low humming again as the narrator speaks.)

Narrator

And Pocahontas, the Indian maid and guardian angel of Jamestown—she whose spirit abides there forevermore. Through the tragedy of pain and suffering and denial of her own race she gave her love and devotion and finally her life that the colony might be saved. Out of the dust of her gentle side, O remember, the flower of freedom blooms.

> (The chorus with a burst of intense bright harmony salutes her as she comes forward and joins the other protectors around Jefferson, and together they drive avid Death from her prey.)

CHORUS

Sing, sing, sing! All hail, hail, hail!

(*As the music and the singing continue, the guardian ghostly figures move implacably and in one will against the skulking figure of Death. She retreats before their influence, her voluminous cloak spasmodically convulsed. The bright defenders herd her away before them into the darkness at the right. At the moment of their disappearance after her there is again a rumble as if underground, followed by a bright flash of lightning at the rear. The chorus stops singing and the greenish light disappears from the scene, leaving it in shadow, with Jefferson now leaning back against the tower in a half-sitting position, his face lifted upward in the night. The light brightens somewhat on him. The narrator continues from the darkness.*)

NARRATOR

Thus in the hour of defeat this mystic affirmation came to Jefferson—a refreshment of his soul—brought to him by the burning and re-awakened image in his heart of those who through great tribulation had washed their robes in the blood of their life's sacrifice and now stood eternal and secure as defenders of the faith for which he fought—and which we the living here tonight have so bountifully inherited.

(*Jefferson springs to his feet.*)

JEFFERSON

(*Vibrantly, joyously.*)
Hugh! Hugh!
(*But there is no answer from the sleeping man. He looks about him, and as if feeling he is on holy ground, pulls off his hat and sinks to his knees in silent prayer. A moment passes, and Cephus enters at the right front. He stops astounded, then likewise takes off his hat. Jefferson looks out at him and quietly rises.*)
Your captain is sleeping. See to him.

CEPHUS

(*Saluting.*)
Aye, aye, I will, sir.

JEFFERSON

You did not desert us, Cephus.

CEPHUS

(*Replacing his hat.*)
Me desert? Not I.

JEFFERSON

I will send a carriage for the captain later. Stand on guard here. We'll get more men.
(*Cephus straightens up.*)
You're a brave soldier and Virginia will remember you.
(*He touches Cephus on the shoulder and goes swiftly away. Cephus, ragged as he is, stands at smart salute, holding his arm across his stomach to retain a bulky object hidden there. He gazes after Jefferson.*)

Cephus

(Finally and a little crowingly.)
Cephus, my lad, hah, hah—the governor hisself—twict now he says you're a brave man.
> *(He walks up and down across the scene, most military-like, but keeping one hand on the bulge under his coat.)*

Stand on guard, he says. Ahm, the whole fort in my charge. But as it says in the great book, the first shall be last and the last first. And from standing tied in the stocks of Williamsburg, I have riz high in the world.
> *(As he marches.)*

But odd's flints and locks, it comes natural in the family. My great, great, great, great, great, great-granddaddy, Michael Sicklemore, was one of the first colonists here and died of the bloody flux so 'tis said—poor fellow—in the year nine—
> *(He looks off appraisingly in the direction Jefferson has gone.)*

—him that was sent south to find Sir Walter Raleigh's Lost Colony and found but a little yaller-haired boy crying in the wilderness.
> *(He glances warily off again and then tiptoes over and sets his gun against the tower.)*

Captain Taylor. He, he, he. When he wakes up—hee-hee—I'll have something to surprise him.
> *(He reaches under his coat.)*

I stepped over to the Jacqueline house—I got us a chicken.
> *(He pulls out a dead chicken, shakes it limberly in the air, and sits down. He begins plucking it, chuckling the while.)*

In peace they shut you up for stealing. In war they call you brave man. Hah-hah-hah!

THE COMMON GLORY

(The organ feels indulgent toward the old thief and strikes a little chord. Cephus lifts his voice in song as he plucks away at the chicken, the organ filling in with accompaniment under him.)

My love she wrung her little hands and cried,
Her hair hung down like a widowed bride,
   She's locked her heart with a golden key,
   A silver chain and a golden key,
To keep it all safe inside.

Saying, "When you come back from the wars **again**,
I'll set it free from its prison pain,
   I'll put your head on my loving breast,
   Your aching head on my sweet loving **breast**,
Where the little key has lain."

(Shaking his head.)

All under and under the leaves of life,
The sparrow scratched for to find him a wife—

(*He goes on whistling the tune as the scene fades out and the light comes up on the narrator.*)

Narrator

With renewed faith Jefferson continued to carry the struggle on. And in the months ahead he had little more than that faith to sustain him. For the people grew more and more reactionary, rebellious and divided. And finally the legislature refused cooperation altogether. Then invasion came. In vain Jefferson tried to rally arms and men against the enemy. In vain he rode and preached and pleaded and persuaded. Now it seemed all was lost.

And in London the news was received with triumph. Certainly the end of the long struggle was near, and the cause of right had won.

(*The light fades from the narrator and comes up on the right side stage.*)

SCENE 5

The inner council of the king's palace. A small richly-furnished room with ornate walls and pilasters and a door framed by two windows at the back. Here the king is sitting behind a long table with some six or eight of his privy council members, among them Lord North. A long plumed pen and inkstand are in front of him. He wears spectacles, the man of documents and business of state now. A paper held aloft in his hand is trembling with his joy and excitement.

KING GEORGE

(*Tearfully.*)
This is the end, gentlemen. The rebels are beaten!
(*Almost shrilly.*)
This late message from General Clinton finally confirms me in it.

VOICES

Hear! Hear!

KING GEORGE

(*Lifting his eyes piously.*)
Almighty God be praised!
(*Emphasizing the air with the document.*)
Now ye see, my faithful ones, how mad it was to talk of peace. Our persistence, our determination have won, and the empire shall not be broken.
(*The tears begin seeping plenteously into his eyes. Half-overcome, he hands the document to North, who looks at it.*)

North

Clinton reports Washington's forces still oppose him.

King George

(*Snapping.*)
Weak forces. Read the message aright—*weak—weak*.
   (*With handkerchief to his face, he stabs at the document with his finger.*)

North

Benedict Arnold has swept up the James River. Richmond, the new capital, is burned.

King George

Ah-ha! Listen, listen!
   (*His shoulders shake with happy sobs.*)

North

The legislature and the traitor Governor Jefferson have fled to the west.

King George

(*Bobbing his head.*)
Aye, aye, and troops under Colonel Tarleton have been dispatched to capture him.
   (*Lifting a clenched fist.*)
And he will be, he will be, and shall stand here—
   (*He whams the table with his big pudgy fist.*)
—in chains to receive his judgment of death from my lips!

Voices

(*Cheering.*)
Bravo! Bravo! Hear! Hear!

OTHER VOICES

Long live the king!
  (*The organ sounds a flourish and begins the martial air "Rule Britannia." The king stands up and starts leading the procession from the scene. A messenger enters swiftly and hands him a paper. He looks at it, then whirls around and holds up the message, controlling the gush of his emotion.*)

KING GEORGE

By swift courier ship.
  (*He reads the message and cries out.*)
Our most loyal Lord Cornwallis has captured Williamsburg! Virginia has fallen!

VOICES

Virginia has fallen!

KING GEORGE

  (*His hand still raised.*)
And the mighty Earl with the flower of the British army now occupies—
  (*Impressively.*)
—the impregnable heights of—Yorktown!

VOICES

Yorktown! Yorktown!

OTHER VOICES

Victory, victory! Long live England!
  (*The king turns and clasps Lord North hysterically and suffocatingly to his bosom. Now his whole form shakes with weeping. The scene blacks out, and the light comes up on the narrator again.*)

Narrator

Whether the occupation of Yorktown by Cornwallis was an answer to Jefferson's prayer or one of the strangest accidents in history—is not for us to say. But it seemed there was a breath-taking possibility that Jefferson's once half-glimpsed vision might come true. Washington clearly saw the chance—but it was maybe one in a million. He decided to take it, and under cover of darkness he got his small army across the Hudson and set out marching rapidly south from New York, the French General Rochambeau and his troops with him. Admiral De Grasse from the West Indies made another gamble and dashed across to enter the Capes in blockade against the British. Lafayette and Anthony Wayne hurried their troops around below the James River to cut off a retreat to the south. And now the ragamuffin American militia—loyal ones and even many of those who had deserted—swarmed in from all sides to join their comrades.

(*The organ sounds a flourish.*)

In from the Albemarle country they came.

(*The organ strikes up "The Westmorland Hunt" tune again, and we hear a chorus of men's rough voices off at the left front. The light fades down on the narrator and rises along the proscenium wall at the left. Here we see a party of some half-dozen men or more in tattered and ill-matched American uniforms stepping briskly down toward the center stage. They are singing lustily as they march.*)

Men

>Today our banners wave on high,
>The drum beats loud, the bugles cry—
>And freedom's men go forth to die,
>   Lead on to victor-ee!

Narrator

(*From the shadow.*)
And from the hills of the river Dan they came.
> (*The group at the left turns into the center stage. The light now comes up along the right proscenium wall and reveals another group of raggle-taggle American militia marching swiftly down. This group carries a high-held American flag as they sing away.*)

Men

(*Loudly.*)
> Hark on the air
> Our guns declare
> In shot and shell—
> The Tories' knell.

Narrator

(*As before.*)
And from the south they came—from Carolina's Currituck country and from Suffolk and Smithfield and Surrey.
> (*The light comes up in a long narrow illumination in front of the left side stage, and here a third group is seen marching toward the center stage, coming out and from behind the left light tower. The second group is now arriving on the rear center stage and joining the first group.*)

Third Group

(*Singing.*)
> Fight—fight—undo them!
> With butt and blade charge through them—
> (*They march straight on toward the center stage.*)

Narrator

(*Again as before.*)

And from the garrisons along the James River—from Hampton, from the Eastern Shore and from old Jamestown.

(*The light fades out from behind the third group and comes up along the path in front of the right side stage. Here a fourth group of marching militia is moving straight ahead, their Virginia flag held aloft. Hugh Taylor is at the head of them and Cephus and Sergeant Jack come close behind.*)

Fourth Group

To England's shores pursue them
And America shall yet be free!
(*With Cephus' great voice bellowing in the lead.*)
Fight—fight—with butt and blade!

(*They march on toward the right rear to join the other groups which are now lining up, all continuing to mark time and singing together. As they sing they gaze expectantly off at their right as if awaiting the appearance of some person or event. The light fades out behind the fourth group and rises in a great gray horizontal column across the rear of the center stage. Townspeople—men, women, and children—have begun to gather excitedly there as on a street or roadway. They too are looking expectantly off.*)

Narrator

(*From the shadow.*)

And here in Williamsburg the people gathered—a day long to be remembered—September 14, 1781. General George Washington and his French allies reached the village in their move to the final attack on Cornwallis at Yorktown.

(*A murmur runs through the people on the center stage.*)

Soldiers and People

(*In a sudden and great cheering call.*)
Washington! General Washington!

(*Then a hush like the stillness of death comes over the scene. A rhythmic low drum beat begins in the organ, above which rises a high fifing call. Two drummers enter along the street from the left rear beating their drums. They march straight ahead of them, their faces set almost like puppets, moving doggedly as of long days and years toward an appointed but never accomplished goal. Behind them come several flagbearers, one carrying the Stars and Stripes, another the Virginia flag and a third, the flag of France. People are taking off their hats now and standing at attention. Here and there women are seen weeping in happiness, and the little children look on with great round eyes as General Washington enters. He is followed by an entourage consisting among others of Lieutenant-Colonel Alexander Hamilton, General Lafayette, the Count de Rochambeau and General Steuben. They are all weary and travel-stained. Washington tall and grave and battle-worn acknowledges with bared head the murmurs and almost silent heart out-pourings of the people on either side. He nods here and there as he moves along. Behind the generals comes a single white horse saddled and bridled and led by an orderly. This is Washington's steed. Next we see a small group of staff officers. And following them come several lusty fellows with ropes looped around*

THE COMMON GLORY

their shoulders, pulling an old clacking field piece heavily along. Other soldiers are pushing it. Following this come the columns of infantry. Our four groups of militiamen begin falling in with them and marching off. Washington and his entourage are now passing out at the right rear. Suddenly the organ switches from its drum beat to "The Westmorland Hunt" tune again, and the people as if breaking from a spell burst into cheers once more, waving their hats and handkerchiefs.)

People

(In wild and long-drawn cries.)
Washington, Washington! General Washington!
(The scene blacks out, and the light comes up on the narrator again.)

Narrator

And day by day on all the roads that converged like spokes toward the hub of a wheel—Yorktown being that hub—the patriots moved. Washington and his generals and the men likewise sensed now the coming immortal event, the final goal. But the way to it would be long and slow and costly and would require patience as they well knew. But then for seven years they had learned to be patient. And doggedly and unrelentingly but with elation and hope in his heart Washington began the siege.

And up at Monticello a committee from the house of delegates waited upon Thomas Jefferson in one of his darkest hours.

(The light fades from the narrator and comes up on the left side stage in an eye-glimpse scene representing a room in Monticello. The furniture is of the simplest. At the back in shadow is a window set

in a paneled wall and draped in tasteful curtains. Jefferson is seated in a chair in the middle of the room, his gaunt figure upright and dour as four committee men stand before him. The first man is reading from a paper he holds in his hand.)

First Man

It has been shown that due to the governor's negligence the legislature was shamefully scattered and barely escaped capture at the hands of Colonel Tarleton. Further, it has been proved no adequate post riders had been established to keep the people informed of the movement of the traitor Arnold. No proper courier service had been provided between the capitol and General Washington. In failing to call out the militia in time his excellency allowed the enemy to invade the commonwealth at will, burning and destroying.

Jefferson

(In a low angry voice.)
There was no militia available sufficient to meet the enemy and you well know it.

Second Man

Right, right. Even as we warned and prayed you a year ago not to dispatch them all away.
(Jefferson gestures irritatedly.)

Jefferson

I acted as I felt best.

Third Man

(Sarcastically.)
Feelings are a poor guide in military matters, sir. It takes—

Jefferson

Intelligence. Of which I have none and you gentlemen have all.

First Man

—And finally it is herewith set forth, sir, that you do stand in full responsibility for the over-running and despoilation of the commonwealth of Virginia. Therefore it is ordered that the said Thomas Jefferson, late governor of Virginia, shall be required to present himself at the next session of the legislature to answer in full and particular these the charges against him.
(*He bows, folds up the paper and puts it into his pocket.*)

Jefferson

(*Quietly, coldly.*)
I shall be there.
(*He bows his head.*)

First Man

Come, gentlemen.
(*They turn away. A scream is heard from a distant part of the house. It is repeated. Jefferson springs to his feet. The door at the rear bursts open and Aunt Nancy rushes in. She seizes Jefferson's arm frantically.*)

Aunt Nancy

Come, Massa Jefferson, come. Something done happen! Oh, my baby lamb. Oh—Oh—She's dying, she's dying!
(*A great shudder goes through Jefferson. He staggers as if about to fall, then whirls and hurries through the door at the rear. Aunt Nancy turns*

fiercely on the men, her voice whining in sobbing fury.)
You done kill her! You done kill her with your shame— you low down trash!

  (She spits viciously at them. Wailing, she flings her apron up to her face and goes out after Jefferson. The sensitive organ begins a low wailing in its turn and continues for a moment.)

  (The men have looked about them, and then moved silently out at the right front as the organ played. The light fades from the scene and comes up on the narrator. The organ stops.)

Narrator

Meanwhile the blockade of Cornwallis at Yorktown was complete. But that wily commander had intrenched himself to stand a long siege behind his breastworks and strong points. One of the most strategic of these strong points controlled the road to Williamsburg. The honor of storming it fell to Lieutenant-Colonel Alexander Hamilton, and with him Major Hugh Taylor. This seemed an unimportant action as compared to many a world battle, but rarely has a greater result depended on the outcome.

(The light fades from the narrator and comes up dimly on the center stage.)

SCENE 6

The battlefield at Yorktown, night, with the enemy redoubt in the right rear, muffled and ominous. The wall of the redoubt has a gap in it showing the ugly muzzle of a squat British cannon. From the redoubt rises a tall staff with a British flag on it. The organ strikes up a cheery fifing marching melody.

 Entering from the right front in the gloom come a cortege of British redcoats, their harness and gear and guns glimmering in the moonlight as they march swiftly along. Half-way across the stage they turn sharply to the left and move back into the shadow. We see now from the top of the parapet the forms of one or two other British soldiers on the lookout. They sink slowly behind their protecting wall. The British reinforcements begin clambering up the redoubt bank, from the front and from the rear. In a moment they have all hidden themselves within its enclosure.
 Here and there off deep and in the distance is heard the intermittent boom of a siege cannon. The British march tune dies out, the booming continues low, wide-spaced and threatening. A moment passes, we see a lookout British soldier again raising his head and shoulders up

above the parapet of the redoubt and then sinking slowly down again. The organ begins a slow legato and monotonous drumbeat—tiresome and irritating in its way, like the drop, drop of water from a faucet. It continues until the audience is not only irritated but expectant.

Entering from the left front out of the shadow come a group of American soldiers. They are creeping stealthily along, their bayoneted muskets held at the ready in front of them. They spread out noiselessly toward the rear.

At the same time entering from the right center come another group of American soldiers. There is a warning flurry of sound in the organ, the men stop still and crouch down. In the pale moonlight glimmering on the redoubt, we see the sentry looking out again. As his figure disappears, the American soldiers resume their approach. The drumbeat in the organ gets a little louder, more ominous—ta-roomp, roomp-roomp—ta-roomp-roomp-roomp. Above the insistent and loudening drumbeat there rises the treble of the organ in a weird little fife-like call repeated again and again.

The American soldiers are converging now on the redoubt. Suddenly the British lookout discovers them.

A gun booms loudly and near at hand in the organ. At this, as if a signal, the American soldiers storm the redoubt. The British soldiers rise up from within and fight back. A bombardment begins now—with heavy guns, the rattle of musketry and the yelling of men as they fight.

The scene is lighted up from bursting shells, and in the flashes, like creatures in a lurid nightmare dream, we see the hand-to-hand mixing and turmoiling and fighting on the redoubt. Here an American falls and tumbles down the wall into the fosse. There a redcoat falls likewise. The battle continues ferociously between these two handfuls of men grappling and hacking and clubbing and stabbing one another—in the swirls and whoomings of light.

The fiercest point of the fighting is around the British flag. Hugh Taylor is seen wresting it from the flag bearer and tearing it down to earth. Cephus rushes up with the American flag which is set in its stead. The Britishers who are left alive flee behind the parapet and beyond. And the victorious Americans now raise a cheer, as their flag flutters in the breeze.

All

(Led by Alexander Hamilton.)
'Ray! 'Ray!
(The cannonading and musketry begin dying away. A last parting shot sounds—whee-oom—and we see Hugh Taylor suddenly stagger. He reaches blindly into the air as if for help, then goes down on his knees and then in the diminishing flashes of light—like the ending of a sudden surging summer storm—we see Cephus and Hamilton bearing him down from the parapet to the shadows below. The cannonading ceases, and the light comes up again on the narrator.)

Narrator

After this redoubt was taken the way was open for the advance on the enemy. Day by day, hour by hour the French and American forces crept relentlessly forward under the shelter of the parallel breastworks thrown up by the engineers. The situation of Cornwallis was now hopeless. The news of his plight came to Robert Gordon in Williamsburg gaol, and that great Tory leader saw at last the ending of his dream. His cause was lost. In a final gesture of defiance and despair he took his own life. The legend goes that the stain of his blood can be seen there on the floor of the gaolhouse to this day. The brokenhearted Eileen buried her father in Bruton Parish Churchyard, and with other Williamsburg women went forth as a nurse among the suffering and dying soldiers.

Hugh Taylor had been seriously wounded and removed to a farmhouse just out of shellfire there close to Yorktown. A few days later our friend Cephus, mixing too close with a Hessian soldier received his scratch of honor on the battlefield and likewise was invalided into this same farmhouse.

(*The light fades from the narrator and comes up on the front center stage.*)

SCENE 7

The interior of a farmhouse—a sort of half-basement room from which the furniture has been removed. About the earthen floor are a number of flat bunches of wheat straw for bedding. Some three or four soldiers are lying around on the straw and in the shadows. Back in the murky gloom at the rear of the scene is a rough plank cot on which a dying Hessian soldier lies. Eileen Gordon is seated by him bathing his face with a damp cloth which she dips into a bucket on the floor. Her face is pale, her eyes hollow from sleeplessness and suffering, and her movements are dulled and heavy, as if her senses and her whole soul were in the grip of some frozen grief or pain. In the right of the scene somewhat close to the footlights sits Hugh Taylor, reclining in a rocking-chair, his haggard face turned and watching Eileen. He is wearing his old service coat by one sleeve, the other one loose and hanging back behind him, leaving the wound between his shoulders and neck free. His chest is bandaged diagonally across and loosely down and under his left arm, though now he has slipped the bandage aside awaiting the dressing. Over at the left we dimly discern the form of Cephus lying on some straw on the floor. His face is buried down on an old pillow or folded blanket, and his rump is stuck a bit comically and coolingly up in the air. He is apparently snoozing away. Eileen finishes with the Hessian and comes over to Hugh with a bottle in her hand. He looks up at her eagerly. She begins bathing Hugh's shoulder with the fiery liquor. He winces under the crawling pain.

HUGH

Brandy is mighty healing for a hurt—the doctors say.
   (*Eileen nods mechanically.*)

EILEEN

Yes.

HUGH

But Cephus there—
   (*He gestures toward the recumbent figure.*)
—has complained bitterly at the waste of it.
   (*He wipes the clammy sweat from his forehead with his free hand. In the distance we hear the intermittent boom of the cannon. Eileen slides the bandage up and over the wound and replaces the folds of the loose coat about him. She turns away to her duties with the other soldiers, but Hugh fervently takes her hand. She stands straight and waiting beside him. He smiles at her.*)
It's still like being in a dream—that you are here.

EILEEN

(*Murmuringly.*)
A dream—
   (*She lifts a hand to her forehead as if to rub away a deep and compelling ache there.*)

HUGH

Here I was that night—lying on the straw half crazy with pain, ready to die. And then—there you were.

EILEEN

The wounded and the dying, Hugh—the sick and suffering.

Hugh

You've saved my life—such as it is—with your nursing.

Eileen

(*Shuddering.*)
The blood, the blood. Will it never end? Will it?

Hugh

(*Soothingly.*)
Soon it will. It can't last but a few more days. And you must rest—please. —On your feet day and night.
(*He half rises out of his chair to give her his seat, but she pushes him back. The Hessian boy moans in the shadows, and she turns back to him. The door at the rear opens and Sergeant Jack comes in. He walks with the aid of a single-stemmed crutch. He sits down on an old stool in the middle background in front of the Hessian's cot.*)

Sergeant Jack

Well, there's news for you—right between the eyes.
(*He flings out his hands in a disgusted gesture.*)

Hugh

Yes?

Sergeant Jack

They say General Clinton's ships have been sighted off the Capes.

Hugh

(*With a groan.*)
Then Cornwallis may escape us yet.
(*Shaking off his apprehension with a quick effort.*)
They say, they say. It's but another rumor.

Sergeant Jack

(*Despondently.*)
You can't beat 'em—them British.
(*He leans his head over on his arms.*)
Seven long years—and you can't beat 'em.

Hugh

(*Vehemently.*)
We can and we will. General Washington will.
(*He makes a sudden start in his chair, then sits writhing with pain and helplessness.*)
We ought to be out there helping.

Sergeant Jack

Much help we'd be—we and the other thousands of disabled and sick.
(*The Hessian boy moans again. Eileen bends over him, smoothing his forehead with the rhythmic stroking of her hand. Sergeant Jack gestures behind him.*)
He can't last much longer, poor fellow. Ah, listen at them guns.
(*He reaches behind him and picks up an object from the boy's cot and holds it in the air, looking at it. It is a silver flute.*)
He was good on that flute.
(*Bitterly.*)
To be hired out, sent here to die three thousand miles from his German home—for a cause he had no interest in.

Hugh

Be mindful of that flute. It's to be sent to Mr. Jefferson.

Sergeant Jack

So.

Hugh

And his music too. He was once a prisoner up there at Charlottesville out of Burgoyne's army before he was exchanged. He and Mr. Jefferson played together, violin and flute—said he loved Mr. Jefferson—he was kind to him.

Sergeant Jack

Mr. Jefferson was better at making music than running a war.

Hugh

(*Angrily.*)
He did all that a human being could do. You couldn't ask more.
(*Eileen comes out of the shadow with a bucket on her arm. Sergeant Jack climbs to his feet.*)

Eileen

I will get fresh water from the spring. He's burning up with a fever.

Sergeant Jack

I'll get it for you, ma'm.
(*Without answering she hurries out at the left front. Sergeant Jack stands looking after her.*)
Work, work. Something's driving her on—like it's killing her.

Hugh

(*Irritatedly, as he lifts his old cudgel from the floor.*)
Aye, grief, grief. Did you ever hear the word? Her

father's dead. She can't forget him. Aih, Lord, if I could help her!
> (*His breath goes out in a great sigh. He strikes the side of his chair with the cudgel. Cephus stirs and crawls up on his knees.*)

CEPHUS

(*Irately.*)
Jabber, jabber, jabber.
> (*He gapes and yawns.*)

HUGH

(*Abstractedly.*)
How are you this morning, Cephus?

CEPHUS

(*Feeling his hindquarters delicately with his finger.*)
Nohow, nohow.

SERGEANT JACK

I dressed his wound awhile ago—hah—wound—nothing but a scratch. And the way he yowled!
> (*He chuckles grimly. Cephus hits the floor a blow with his old three-cornered hat.*)

CEPHUS

I'll have ye to know many a man has died with less. A scratch, heh? That there Hessian boy had a scratch when I took him prisoner—and now he's mortified—look at him.

SERGEANT JACK

(*Mollifyingly.*)
Aye, Cephus, aye.

HESSIAN BOY

(*Suddenly from the shadow.*)
Mutti! Mutti!

CEPHUS

What's he saying now?

HUGH

"Mutti, mutti." He's calling for his mother.

CEPHUS

Mutti, mutti! What kind of quare talk is that? She couldn't understand him.
(*The sergeant turns back to the boy's cot.*)

SERGEANT JACK

(*From the shadows, softly in bad German.*)
Zuruck schnell—she kommen schnell.
(*Cephus rises warily to his feet and rests his back against the wall of the room. We understand now that he has been wounded slightly in the rear. He feels himself gently and appraisingly and lets out a howl as if stricken with torture.*)

CEPHUS

Ee—yow!
(*Muttering as Hugh and Sergeant Jack break out in a sudden rough laugh.*)
Ah, but I paid that redcoat back. The minute he cut me so—I whirled and kerdab I spet a charge of Virginia 'baccer juice slam in his eyes. And then when I had him blinded so, I give him the quietus—hum—hum—with my muskit butt I did so—and left him cold in death.
(*Hugh is now resting his hands and chin on his cudgel, gazing out before him.*)

Hugh

I heard he got up and ran away.

Cephus

Ah-hah! Backbiting and evil tongues forevermore!
  (*Piteously.*)
But so it is that other good men be persecuted in the godless days of this bassackward world.

Sergeant Jack
  (*Jocosely.*)
Who, Cephus?

Cephus

The great Thomas Jefferson hisself for one and the same. Ahm, him and me both together are of the same pair alike—downtrodden, spet upon, and misused by the commonwealth of this state.

Hugh

True about Mr. Jefferson all right. It's a tragedy how they've used him.

Cephus
  (*Incredulously.*)
Tragedy! It's the worst bad manners in the world.
  (*He wipes his eyes.*)
They've killed him off, that's what they have—broke his heart slam in two.

Hugh

Not Thomas Jefferson! He'll fight on—never quit—he and General Washington. Fight till this republic is won.

Cephus

Aye.
   (*Blowing his nose with a great snort.*)
And I wisht they'd hurry and win it myself. I wish so, you hear me.
   (*With contemplative self-pity.*)
But who cares for the wants and wishes of poor Cephus Sicklemore—nobody—not a single solitary soul.
   (*Angrily.*)
Do they honor me for my bravery? No. Do they attend me in my condition? No.
   (*He tramps limpingly about—then savagely.*)
Down with women, say I!

Hugh

So, Cephus?

Cephus

   (*Scathingly.*)
So. And well ye might say the same.
   (*Vehemently.*)
Ye woman is ye monster of iniquity. Slicker than a sarpent, wiser than a dove, and as the scriptures say, in all things whatsoever devious and vile and whose footsteps take hold on—

Sergeant Jack

Whist, Cephus, you're sworn to love.

Hugh

   (*Mockingly quoting.*)
"This time I'm a marrying man sanctified down to the ground"—

Cephus

(*With a squeal.*)
My soul pukes and purges with bile at the name of woman. I could spit vinegar at the name of woman.
  (*He spits. Hugh and Sergeant Jack laugh again. He goes on half-whimperingly.*)
Here I've been, laid up, my blood poured out like a crimson freshet for my country's cause—and not a word, not a whisper, not a pastry have I had!

Sergeant Jack

(*Crowingly.*)
Oh, I see—Mammy Huzzitt.

Cephus

(*Ragingly.*)
Mammy, Mammy—don't mention that creature's name in the sound of my hearing. My two ears shut up like clams before it.
  (*Going on sweetishly.*)
But praise be to Almighty God the surgeons and doctors have took a good care of me—hah, hah, hah. For all that huzzy Huzzitt cares, I might be dead and buried out there with them other poor boys in the cold rotten trenches. Aye, good men they are, them doctors. They feel me kindly and say to me—Cephus, my lad, how are ye, boy? Poorly, says I. I've lost much blood. Good, says his honor the surgeon. Bleed him. And so they take away a cupful of my life's gore. Hah-hah-hah! My manhood calms down and I rest. They come again in the morning, anxious about me. How are you, Cephus, honey lad? they say. Weak, says I, still able to whisper, and nigh to the cooling board I fear. Aye, says his honor, the man with the saws and gimlets and the cupping glass, it's them

vapors filling him with icy fog. Bleed him once more and let the mulligrubs melt and run out. And so they take care of me again and drain me dry as a shuck in winter time—till I can't spit.

(*He spits.*)

Aye, good men they are.

(*He sets himself precariously and dolefully down along the edge of the stool and pats his foot dismally on the floor. He begins to hum to himself from irritation, then finally brings his vocables into song.*)

CEPHUS

(*Half to himself.*)

I'll march to the country that lies in the west, Where a poor soldier lad with good fortune is blest. 'Tis there like old Croesus I'll live at my ease, From the gold in the hills and the fruit on the trees.

(*His voice dies down to humming again.*)

HUGH

(*Looking up.*)

True, Cephus, there is land in the west for the soldiers.

Cephus

Heh?

Hugh

It has been voted—Governor Jefferson saw to that before he gave up office. You can make a home there in the west.

Cephus

(*Thoughtfully.*)
Ahm. And a man mought dig hisself some gold in them hills.
(*Making a swift digging motion.*)
Hanh!

Sergeant Jack

(*With comic scorn.*)
Uh-uh! Cephus—there goes more of your sweated lard.
(*Cephus piteously and with groanings lies down on his straw again. Mammy Huzzitt comes in at the rear with a basket on her arm. She brushes by Hugh without noticing him, her eyes fastened on Cephus. Cephus looks around and up at her as if seeing an apparition. He rises. Mammy Huzzitt stops.*)

Mammy Huzzitt

(*Yearningly.*)
Oh, Cephus!
(*Cephus' face undergoes a transformation.*)

Cephus

Ah, my lovely, the moon and the stars they shine again.

Mammy Huzzitt

Soon as I heard you were wounded, my poor hero, I hurried here.

CEPHUS

Ah, wonderful, wonderful. Listen to her. My honey-love, my sugar-bunch—sweet, sweet. And the pastries?
(*He moves forward to meet her, limping as he does so. Mammy Huzzitt cries out.*)

MAMMY HUZZITT

Poor lad! Is your leg broke, Cephus? Did they wound you in your sweet pitiful leg?

CEPHUS

(*Clearing his throat.*)
Ahm, ahm—
(*He reaches for the pastry basket, but she lifts it away.*)

MAMMY HUZZITT

Show me, Cephus, show me.

CEPHUS

The pastries, the pastries.
(*He steps forward and Mammy Huzzitt reaches to pluck him back. She touches his sore place, and Cephus lets out a howl, his hand instinctively flying to protect his wounded spot behind. Then he tries quickly to establish it elsewhere by grabbing his leg with both hands and moaning.*)
Oh my knee, my destroyed knee!
(*Mammy Huzzitt's eyes blink. She peeps around, then straightens up stiffly.*)

MAMMY HUZZITT

A-hah! And how did that happen?

Cephus

(*Piteously.*)
Oh my turtle dove, my mockingbird, my lark!
(*He reaches out his great hands to her.*)

Mammy Huzzitt

And me all night, weeping and hurrying the long road from Williamsburg and calling out, "Cephus, Cephus!" to all the trees and the fences that I passed—the woods behind me echoing with the name "Cephus, my love, my hero!"
(*Sternly.*)
And how did you get yourself wounded there!

Cephus

I was surrounded, I tell you. While I fou't 'em off in front, they come at me aft.

Mammy Huzzitt

(*Weepishly.*)
Oh, Cephus—you're still a coward!
(*Sergeant Jack comes back out of the shadow and sits down on his stool, his head bent over.*)

Hugh

(*Indulgently.*)
I vouch for him. He's a brave and loyal man. I so declare it.
(*Mammy Huzzitt relents a little, and Cephus makes for her to enfold her with one arm and dig into the pastry basket with the other. But she backs quickly away and stands appraising him. Her face softens and she gestures leadingly toward the exit.*)

Mammy Huzzitt

My Cephus—sweet Cephus....
(She clucks tolingly to him.)

Cephus

(Hasselling with hunger.)
Pastries—pastries!
(Mammy Huzzitt keeps backing away to the door, leading him on. He follows her into the doorway and then starts back with an exclamation.)
Uh-uh!
(Fiercely.)
A preacher!—She's got a preacher out there!
(He peers off.)
My heart hardens—

Mammy Huzzitt

(Piteously.)
Cephus, Cephus.
(She shakes the pastry basket at him.)
I got a good wagon of straw waiting to take you back to Williamsburg. And a soft feather bed there calling to you. And I'll smoothe your forehead, Cephus, my lamb, and rub you and tend to you.
(She comes purringly up to him, still holding the basket out of his reach.)
But first the preacher must marry us, honey—I'm determined.
(She shakes the basket at him again and strokes his face. A terrific struggle is going on in Cephus. It is now that the long servitude to his belly proves his undoing. He begins to yield.)

CEPHUS

(*Whispering.*)
Marry, the Good Book says—marry and give in marriage—

MAMMY HUZZITT

Aye, Cephus, aye. Once ye do it, it's not so bad.

HUGH

(*Calling out.*)
You're a hero, Cephus. Now rise up and be a man. Marry the woman.
(*Cephus still stands battling within himself.*)

CEPHUS

(*Finally.*)
Be that an order, major?

HUGH

As your commanding officer—it is.

CEPHUS

Hum—
(*He reaches for the pastry basket. Mammy Huzzitt keeps it just out of reach, leading him on. He succumbs. He echoes as they go.*)
Soft feather bed—soft feeling woman—
(*They go out up the steps at the rear. Sergeant Jack moves over to the door and peers after them. He carries the flute in his hand. Suddenly he lifts it to his lips and plays a saluting skirl to the off-stage scene.*)

SERGEANT JACK

(*Presently.*)
They're holding hands. The preacher's standing in front

of them and she's feeding Cephus pastries like fish to a seal.

(*Yelling off suddenly.*)

Kiss the bride, Cephus, kiss her!

(*One or two of the wounded soldiers around in the straw stir and mutter in irritation. Eileen comes in with a bucket of water from the right front. She goes over to the cot where the Hessian boy lies.*)

Eileen

Bitte, mein kind.

(*A moment passes and she comes slowly out of the shadows. Hugh looks up at her inquiringly. She murmurs.*)

He's dead.

(*She stands swaying with weakness.*)

And I was not here.

(*Hugh gets out of his chair and makes his way to her. He puts his arm around her to keep her from falling.*)

Hugh

He's out of his pain now. Poor fellow. It's better so.

(*He starts leading her toward the rocking-chair. Suddenly a tremendous bedlam of bugles begins going in the distance, followed by shouting and yelling. Sergeant Jack looks swiftly out the door at the rear.*)

Sergeant Jack

(*Excitedly.*)

Something's happened. The people are running around like mad out there.

(*A soldier tears in at the right front.*)

SOLDIER

(*Half-hysterically.*)
Cornwallis is beaten! He's beaten!
> (*He runs around the room, waving his hat. Sergeant Jack whirls on him and grabs him fiercely by the shoulders.*)

SERGEANT JACK

(*Loudly.*)
Speak it man! Speak it again.

SOLDIER

He's asked for terms to lay down his arms. Colonel Hamilton has announced it to us. Yay-eeh! Yay-eeh!
> (*He charges out at the left front, shouting as he goes.*)

The war is over! It's over!
> (*Sergeant Jack hurries after him. In the distance now a loud booming of cannon is heard joining in the celebration. The wounded soldiers in the room raise themselves up and give a pitiful cheer. Some of them burst into tears and lie there in the straw weeping happily. Hugh and Eileen stand looking at each other. A moment they stand so. The bugles and yells and booming guns continue outside and far away now.*)

EILEEN

(*Huskily.*)
Listen, listen.
> (*Her face flooding with feeling, the tenseness beginning to pass from her.*)

There'll be no more killing—no more blood—no killing and dying, Hugh. Oh, Hugh!

THE COMMON GLORY 249

(*She bursts into wild sobs and clings vehemently to him. His arms go out and hold her tight against his breast. Presently his voice rises broken and caressing.*)

Hugh

It's all right now—everything will be right now. I'll take care of you—forever, forever. My darling!
(*The scene blacks out and the light comes up on the narrator again.*)

Narrator

The gallant Cornwallis, in order to conserve the lives of his brave men, thus took upon himself the tragedy and shame of surrender, and on October 19, 1781, laid down his arms. The Tory power in America was forever broken, and the colonies had finally won their independence.

But the people were faced with another task as hard as the one they had just finished—the building of their young nation and their government on secure foundations against the challenges and threats of an uncertain future. And there on the bluffs of Richmond one summer day Thomas Jefferson still looked ahead to the future with courage and faith.
(*The light fades out from the narrator and comes up on the full center stage.*)

SCENE 8

An outdoor scene on the bluffs at Richmond. At the right center front is a group of Virginia notables in the colorful dress of the times, and on a rise of ground behind them and off to the side a crowd of citizens, workers, and farmers. There are a few flags and banners in the scene, which is in holiday mood, much the same as at the end of Act I.

Beyond the center of the stage at the left rear, we see some twenty-five or thirty pioneers resting with bundles and baggage on the ground, just as if they had stopped in the scene a moment before proceeding onward. Among these are Hugh Taylor and his wife, Eileen, Mr. and Mrs. Cephus Sicklemore and their four children, now somewhat more grown up than when we saw them last.

When the light comes up on the scene, the people are cheering loudly. Patrick Henry is speaking, but not with the fire and fervor of old. He is now a very sick man. His face is haggard, his eyes large and hollow—his appearance much like old William Pitt himself in a former scene. He is supporting himself with a cane rather than crutches. He lifts his still magic hand, and the cheering dies down.

Henry

We have now just witnessed the victory of our arms—a stroke which means that the cause for which we have bled, suffered and died is secure. And no man more than Thomas Jefferson has helped to bring that eventuality to pass. Without him, ladies and gentlemen, there would

have been no Yorktown. Without him there would have been few of the great documents and principles written forth and produced into being which are now the established law of the land and the guarantees of freedom for generations yet to be.
(Pausing and then simply, as he gestures toward the left.)
Mr. Jefferson.
(Thomas Jefferson comes forward. The people cheer him mightily. Hats are thrown up, handkerchiefs are waved, and the organ declares forth its accustomed welcoming flourish.)

People

(Loudly.)
Jefferson! Jefferson!
(Jefferson is obviously touched by the reception. Like Henry he shows the wear and tear of the years that have gone by and the tribulations through which he has passed. His face is lined and his shoulders a little stooped. But the fire that is in him, the vision that sustains him—they have not weakened. He speaks simply and yet with an undiminished inner passion of belief.)

Jefferson

We are met here today, my friends, on the bluffs of this mighty James River. And in the ashes of this, our little town of Richmond, we now set ourselves to build a capitol. And on this very spot, we have marked out the place for our building—a building which shall be the church, the synagogue, the cathedral—call it what you will—of the truths which we as an independent nation believe in. Here in these lofty hills, in the free air of the great commonwealth of Virginia shall rise the temple and the shelter then of our hope and of our dreams.

We have finished a tragic and terrible war. At this hour let us remember with reverence those our friends who died in it. In the name of their sacrifice, let us here determine that they shall not have died in vain—in frustration and despair.

(*Lifting his hand.*)

And that means, my friends, that we must continue the struggle—not the struggle against an armed enemy—but a struggle against an enemy nevertheless. The enemy of disunion, of selfishness, of greed.

We have declared for the equality of men—for the freedom of men, and we have still another declaration in making these thirteen colonies into one nation—the responsibility of men. For this freedom which we have so bitterly fought for and won can only remain so if we, the servitors and begetters of it, give ourselves as freely to the welfare of the whole. We have established the principle of majority government. It means just that. That each and every man has a responsibility to the will of the majority. And the good of the majority is the duty of the individual. Am I my brother's keeper? I am. And so is he mine. And as we give, so shall we receive. And there can be no true receiving unless there is equal giving. So—matters of public interest are and must be, matters of private responsibility and concern. Only thus can our democracy continue to live and grow strong.

(*His voice vibrant.*)

I believe in the depths of my soul that we have envisioned here in this new land of ours an ideal which if shared throughout the world can bring to that world immeasurable benefits.

(*Gesturing toward the pioneers at the left rear.*)

And you who are marching out to the west—and to the

Ohio—carry with you part of this dream. And as you make your new homes in the new land, clearing the forest, breaking the fresh earth of the prairies, rearing your families—let there be like a blessing running through your days, this American ideal—this dream of freedom, justice and truth among men. On these the brotherhood of man must be based.

(Gesturing at one of the flags near by.)

And this flag here stands as an emblem of our belief, of our credo of government—the flag of free men.

(The organ sounds its flourish again, and the people cheer.)

JEFFERSON

And now Virginia belongs not to herself, but to the nation, even as this our nation shall belong to the world. And the stars in this our flag lighted on high shall be the hopes of men everywhere, and the stripes and bars are our sufferings that we have endured to make these hopes prevail. And I repeat a solemn warning—we must still continue to struggle, continue to fight on and on through the days ahead—

(Moving a bit forward, his eyes lifted out over the audience into the night.)

—through the generations ahead—creating and building and never relaxing our vision—

(Loudly.)

—that our nation may live—that our dream may not die!

(The organ booms out an announcing chord in its marching song. The light begins to die on the center stage at the front, and all the marchers at the center back pick up their bags and start moving away. The organ continues its music.)

ALL THE PEOPLE

(*Singing gaily, accompanied by the organ and the chorus.*)

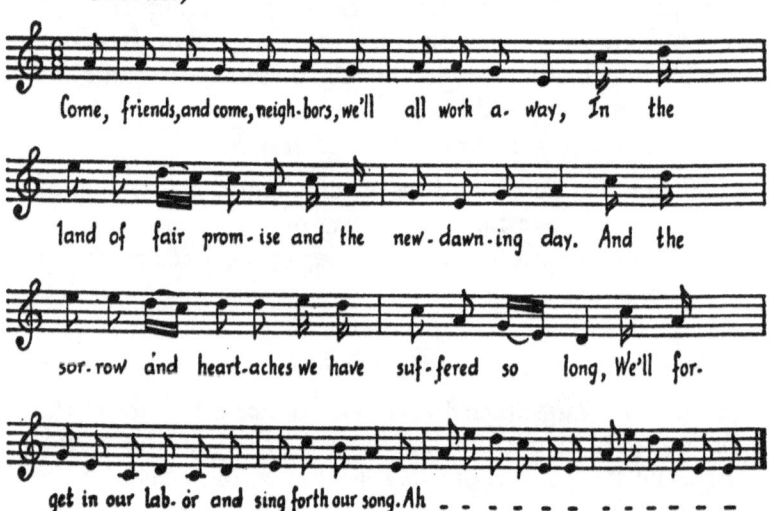

Come, friends, and come, neighbors, we'll all work a-way, In the land of fair prom-ise and the new-dawn-ing day. And the sor-row and heart-aches we have suf-fered so long, We'll for-get in our lab-or and sing forth our song. Ah — — — — — — — —

(*The marchers move on out at the right, and the rest of the people watch them go, waving their handkerchiefs and flags in farewell and continuing the song. Then they too start moving across the scene to the left, returning to their homes. Jefferson stands in the middle of the scene gazing after the pioneers, the sun on his face. A moment he stands so and then turns and goes slowly out at the left front following his neighbors and townsmen. Just as he is beginning to be enveloped in the reaching shadows at the left, the voice of the narrator comes out of the darkness.*)

NARRATOR

And thus this valiant patriot, this wise and good man, passes from our view. And into the wider service of his country he goes. Yea, he passes from the mortality of our sight here tonight into the immortality of a living remembrance—a remembrance as vital and rich today as was his presence on this spot a hundred and seventy-five years ago.

(*The music of the chorus has diminished now into a deep and vibrant humming, accompanied by the low, faint, ground bass of the organ. The singing of the pioneers at the right begins to fade away. The narrator continues.*)

And a thankful and reverent nation has enshrined him forever in its heart!

(*The humming of the chorus strengthens, and the organ comes out a little more dominantly, with a fluty aerial harmony in the high treble keys. And now like a vision we see at the far center back of the stage the gradually appearing and illuminated Jefferson Memorial in Washington City—its tall columns and dome becoming more and more distinct, like something in a dream. And as the wordless harmony pours out through the night like the vast wind among the trees and the organ music shimmers in the air, the interior of the Memorial slowly lights up, and the illumination on the outside fades away. And there we see standing among the columns in the distance the figure of Thomas Jefferson, tall and strong and dark in its eternal bronze. The voice of the narrator sounds again from the shadows.*)

And from the shrine of Thomas Jefferson the ages shall continue to hear the credo of faith—which is our common glory—

(*His voice becomes a huge whisper now but reverent withal, his words seeming to come from the statue itself.*)

"—We hold these truths to be self-evident—that all men

are created equal—that they are endowed by their creator with certain inalienable rights—that among these are life, liberty and the pursuit of happiness—

(*The light on the figure begins to dim.*)

"—that to secure these rights governments are instituted among men, deriving their just powers from the consent of the governed—"

Ah — — — — — — — — — — — Oh, say does that star spang-led ban-ner yet wave, that ban-ner yet wave, O'er the land of the free, O'er the land of the free, O'er the land of the free and the home of the brave!

(*The narrator's sonorous voice dies out, the organ music builds to a climax and the humming of the chorus likewise. The light fades from the Jefferson statue, leaving the Memorial in darkness. The organ begins its shimmering aerial music again, and now surging in as if on its harmony a glowing illumination appears in the sky up and behind the Memorial. Revealed there on its tall flag-pole in a circle of light is the Stars and Stripes, radiant, fluttering and alive. The chorus modulates into a dynamic interpretation of the last few bars of the national anthem. The organ drops down sustainingly under it. The light comes up on the chorus as the chant finishes in* a high exultant harmony with the words—"*And the home of the brave.*" The final chord is held and given all the power of the chorus and the thunder of the organ. Suddenly the music is cut off, the light dies from the chorus and comes up in the amphitheatre. The flag continues its gay fluttering there in the night.)

THE END

MUSIC IN "THE COMMON GLORY"

ACT ONE

Overture............
    (From the "Veni Creator" by J. Farmer, in Thomas Este's *The Whole Book of Psalms*, and an Alman in *Will Forster's Virginal Book*—arranged for the organ by John O'Steen.)

"Out of the Rich and Deep-bosomed Earth"......
Paul Green

    (To a chant by Henry Purcell, *The Hymnal* of the Protestant Episcopal Church, 1940—arranged for The Common Glory Chorus by Carl Fehr.)

"Here in the Silence of These Hills"........Paul Green
    (To a chant by Thomas Tallis in the Episcopal Hymnal, 1940—arranged for The Common Glory Chorus by Carl Fehr.)

"Here's a Health Unto His Majesty".....Jeremy Savile
    (From William Chappell's *Popular Music of the Olden Time*, Vol. 2.)

"Rule Britannia" (King's Entrance Music).......
Thomas Arne

    (From Chappell, Vol. 2.)

"The Staines Morris Tune" (A dance)...........
Traditional English

    (From Chappell, Vol. 1.)

"Alman" (A garden dance).............Anonymous
    (From *Will Forster's Virginal Book*.)

"Sumer Is Icumen In" (A garden dance)..........
                                    13th Century English
   (From Chappell, Vol. 1.)
"We'll Smite The Tories Hip and Thigh"...Paul Green
   (To a traditional English Folk Tune "The Westmorland Hunt" from *English Minstrelsy*, Vol. 2, by Edmondstoune Duncan.)
"Now What Is Love"............Words attributed to
                                    Sir Walter Raleigh
   (Music by Robert Jones and published in his *Second Booke of Ayres*, 1601.)
"Gilderoy"........................Traditional Scotch
   (From *The Songs of Scotland*, edited by Graham, Mudie, etc.)
"Galliard, Sweet Margaret" (festival dance)......
                                    Traditional English
   (From Chappell, Vol. 1.)
"Behold He That Keepeth Israel"........The Psalmist
   (Chant arranged for The Common Glory Chorus by Carl Fehr.)

ACT TWO

Overture............
   (From the Scotch tune "Glenogie" and the English song "Heart of Oak"—arranged for the organ by John O'Steen.)
The Lord's Prayer.............
   (A chant by J. Farmer from Thomas Este's *The Whole Book of Psalms*.)
"Heart of Oak".....................William Boyce
   (From Chappell, Vol. 2.)

"We Dig This Iron"..Melody and words by Paul Green

"Out of the Deep Have I Called"..........W. T. Best
(From the Episcopal Hymnal, 1940—arranged for The Common Glory Chorus by Carl Fehr.)

"Down In Yon Forest," a Christmas Carol.......
Traditional English
(In *Ten Christmas Carols from the Southern Appalachian Mountains.*)

"I Took My Gun And Away To War"
Words and Music by Paul Green

"Irish Ho-Hoane".....................Anonymous
(From the *Fitzwilliam Virginal Book*—arranged for The Common Glory Chorus by Carl Fehr.)

"My Lodging Is On The Cold Ground"..........
Matthew Locke
(From Chappell, Vol. 2.)

"The British Grenadiers"..........Traditional English
(From Chappell, Vol. 1.)

"Glenogie".....................Traditional Scotch
(From *The Minstrelsy of Scotland*, edited by Alfred Moffat.)

In July, 1936, a group of Virginia citizens meet in Williamsburg to consider the production of a Virginia patriotic drama. *Left to right*, William A. Wright, Chairman of the Virginia Conservation Commission; Virginia Waller Davis, Director of the State Departmental News Service; Bela W. Norton, Vice-President in charge of Public Relations for Colonial Williamsburg; S. H. Plummer, Newport News banker; J. C. Harrington, Superintendent of the Colonial National Park at Yorktown; Colgate W. Darden, Jr., former governor of Virginia, now President of the University of Virginia; Channing M. Hall, Mayor of Williamsburg; Albert Sidney Johnson, President of the James River Bridge Corporation; George Prince Arnold, Assistant Commissioner of the Virginia Conservation Commission; C. Wiley Grandy, Norfolk banker; Charles B. Borland, former city manager of Norfolk; Paul Green, playwright, author of *The Common Glory* and *The Lost Colony*; Thomas J. Allen, Regional Director of the National Park Service; Ellen M. Bagby, Chairman of the Jamestown Committee for the Association for the Preservation of Virginia Antiquities. (*Virginia State Chamber of Commerce*)

We wander through the beautiful William and Mary woods in winter looking for a site for our outdoor theatre. (*Virginia State Chamber of Commerce*)

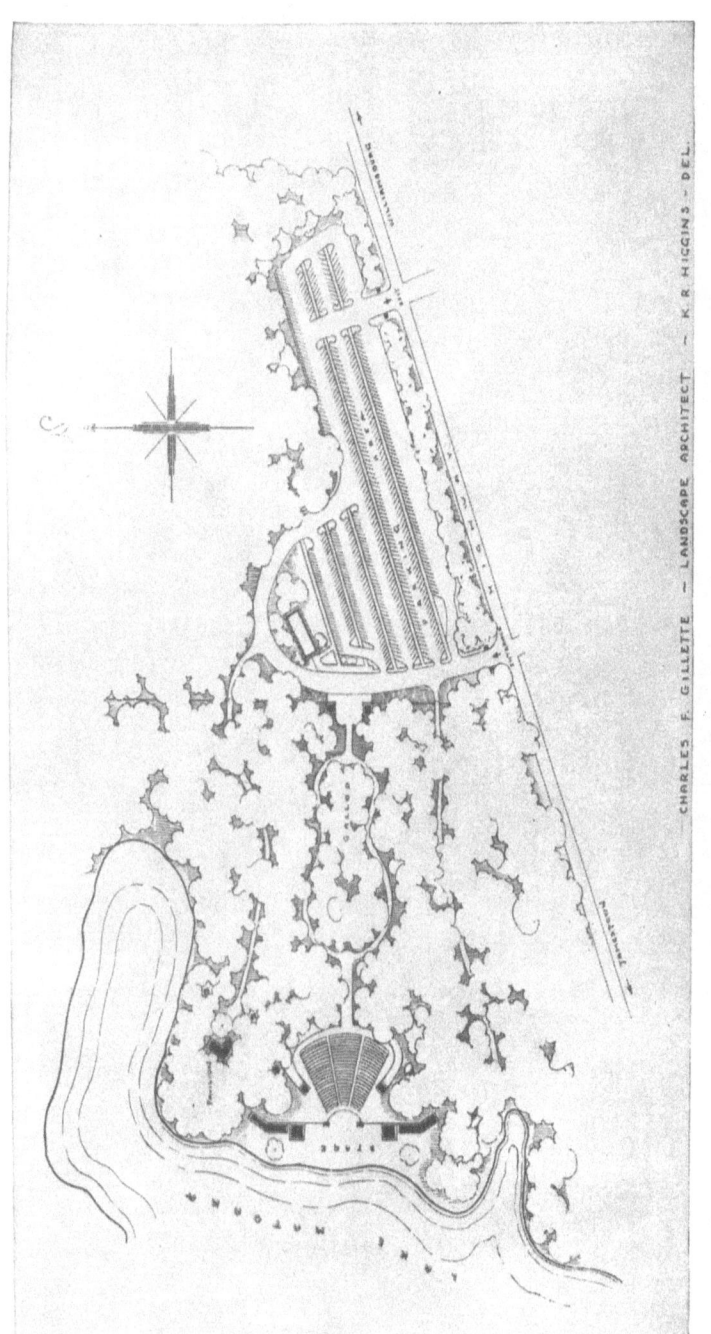

Plan of the theatre and grounds with approaches and parking lot. Charles F. Gillette, landscape architect. (*Williamsburg Photo Service*)

Colonel Charles B. Borland points out how we can save a beloved beech tree. (*Williamsburg Photo Service*)

With the trees cleared and hauled away, the bulldozer starts pushing the earth down toward the stage site. (*Colonial Studios*)

Within a few weeks concrete is laid for the stage floor and the light towers begin rising in the amphitheatre. And ever the Negro rolls his wheelbarrow and swings his pick to help. (*Photo by Steel*)

Noon hour on the project. Our helpers, both prison and union, are back in the shade of the trees eating their lunch. (*Virginia State Chamber of Commerce*)

One hour before the time for opening performance the theatre is swept and cleaned and stands waiting. (*Williamsburg Photo Service*)

John Morley as the Narrator. (*Colonial Studios*)

Mrs. William Byrd (played by Sherry Roberts) reads an old document in a colonial setting. (*Virginia State Chamber of Commerce*)

Thomas Jefferson (played by William W. Smithers) and a comic friend (played by Joseph Buchanan) meet on a winter night at the old Jamestown tower, Act II, Scene 3. (*Williamsburg Photo Service*)

Maria Hunt poses as the dark lady of Jamestown. (*Williamsburg Photo Service*)

"The Common Glory Chorus," Carl A. Fehr conductor, Johnny O'Steen organist. (*Virginia State Chamber of Commerce*)

Between rehearsal calls Robert Gordon (played by Euclid M. Hanbury, Jr.) and Eileen Gordon (played by Evalyn Blandford) take time to do a little fishing in beautiful Matoaka Lake. (*Williamsburg Photo Service*)

Some members of the cast are recorded by the motion picture camera.
(*Williamsburg Photo Service*)

We were blessed with large audiences. Here is one relaxing during the intermission. Part of "The Common Glory Chorus" in the foreground stand up to stretch their legs. The big organ is in the left foreground. (*Williamsburg Photo Service*)

The entire company of "The Common Glory" assemble on the stage to have their picture taken. (*Colonial Studios*)

PROGRAM OF THE FIRST SEASON

THE JAMESTOWN CORPORATION
in coöperation with
THE VIRGINIA CONSERVATION COMMISSION

presents

THE COMMON GLORY

A Symphonic Drama of American History in Two Acts

(WITH MUSIC, PANTOMIME AND DANCE)

by

PAUL GREEN

Directed by

ALTHEA HUNT *and* ROGER BOYLE

MATOAKA LAKE THEATRE
(Beside the Jamestown Road)

WILLIAMSBURG, VIRGINIA

Performances at 8:15 o'clock in the evening, Tuesday through Sunday

JULY 17th THROUGH SEPTEMBER 14th, 1947

Musical Dirctor .... CARL A. FEHR
Scenery and Lighting Designer .... ROGER SHERMAN
Costume Designer .... SUSANNE SHERMAN
Technical Director .... ALBERT HAAK
Stage Manager .... ANTHONY MANZI
Properties .... CLARA BLACK
Dance Director .... MURIEL SHELLEY
Make-Up Designer .... VIRGINIA HARDEN STEWART
Organist ....:.................. JOHN O'STEEN

Production Manager .... THOMAS THORNE
Publicity Director .... VIRGINIA WALLER DAVIS
Executive Vice-President in Charge of
  Construction and Operation .... CHARLES B. BORLAND
Architect and Builder of the Theatre... CHARLES M. MAJOR
Consulting Engineer .... LOUIS C. WILLOUGHBY
Landscape Architect .... CHARLES F. GILLETTE
Sound Equipment Engineer .... WALKER COTTRELL, JR.

CHARACTERS IN THE PLAY

(In the Order of Their Appearance)

Narrator	{ ROBERT DALE MARTIN { RONALD KING
Trumpeters	{ CLARICE GARRISON { HELEN WALKER
Court Dancer	FRANCES BRIGHAM
Major-domo	KENNETH RAND MCGINN
Flag-bearer	JOHN TURNER
King George, III	BRISTOW HARDIN, JR.
Lord North	CLINTON ATKINSON
Spanish Ambassador	JAMES BRAY
French Ambassador	KENNETH LASSITER
Earl of Cornwallis	{ RONALD KING { ARTHUR C. LIVICK, JR.
Robert Gordon	EUCLID M. HANBURY, JR.
Eileen Gordon	EVALYN BLANDFORD
William Pitt	HOWARD SCAMMON
Messenger	ROBERT PACE
Opposition Member	GEORGE ANDERSON
George Mason	WILLIAM C. LARNER
Thomas Jefferson	WILLIAM W. SMITHERS
Benjamin Franklin	REED WHIPPLE
John Adams	REX SATER
Roger Sherman	FELIX HOFFMANN
Robert Livingston	EUGENE BLACK
Samuel Adams	MURRAY L. SHAPIRO
Mrs. Jefferson	DOROTHY LEWIS
Hugh Taylor	DENIS VAUGHAN
Colonel Corbin	NATHANIEL WHITE
Mrs. Corbin	SHERRY ROBERTS
Mrs. Wormley	MARIE HUNT
Mr. Wormley	GEORGE ANDERSON
Nancy Corbin	VIRGINIA JAMES
Francis Corbin	RICHARD OWEN
Cephus Sicklemore	JOSEPH BUCHANAN

PROGRAM OF THE FIRST SEASON

Peter Pelham	Eugene C. Ninde, Jr.
Mammy Huzzitt	Anna Belle Koenig
Town Crier	Mayer Joseph Binder
Sergeant	Arthur C. Livick, Jr.
Patrick Henry	John Manos
Reverend Mr. Madison	Benjamin Bray
Flag-bearer	Robert Lewis
Miss Hallam	Forrestine Whitaker
Martha Carr	Georgia Selph
First Delegate	Shanley Keeter
Second Delegate	William C. Larner
Third Delegate	James Bray
Fourth Delegate	Kenneth Rand McGinn
Death	Marie Hunt
John Smith	Kenneth Lassiter
John Rolfe	Felix Hoffmann
Nathaniel Bacon	{ Ronald King / Mayer Joseph Binder }
Pocahontas	Florence Gaither
Messenger	Richard Owen
Alexander Hamilton	George Anderson
A Hessian Soldier	Rex Sater

Lords at the Court: Mayer Binder, R. R. Boyd, Shanley Keeter, Wilbert Keys, John Manos, Richard Owen, Frank Ryland, Nathaniel White.

Ladies at the Court: Florence Gaither, Marie Hunt, Virginia James, Sherry Roberts, Margaret Rudd, Georgia Selph, Forrestine Whitaker, June White.

Dancing Girls: Nancy Beamer, Caroline Bell, Virginia Bell, Marguerite Bozarth, Mary Frances Faison, Virginia Parthenis.

Members of the Virginia House of Delegates: R. Boyd, Ben Bray, Russell Carlisle, E. M. Hanbury, Jr., Felix Hoffmann, Wilbert Keys, Eugene Ninde, Rex Sater, John Turner.

Townspeople of Williamsburg: Virginia Adair, George Anderson, Clinton Atkinson, Nancy Beamer, Caroline

PROGRAM OF THE FIRST SEASON

Bell, Virginia Bell, Eugene Black, Marguerite Bozarth, James Bray, Russell Carlisle, Jule Dews, Mary Frances Faison, Lore Foltin, Florence Gaither, Clarice Garrison, Mrs. Arthur Gordon, Marie Hunt, Jane Johnson, Shanley Keeter, Wilbert Keys, Ronald King, William Larner, Kenneth Lassister, Mrs. Ernest J. Lee, Kenneth McGinn, Robert Pace, Virginia Parthenis, Grace Raiter, Sherry Roberts, Margaret Rudd, Rex Sater, Georgia Selph, Murray Shapiro, John Turner, Helen Walker, Reed Whipple, June White.

CHILDREN: Nancy Gordon, Hugh Hitchins, Sue Johnson, Barbara Lee, Robert Stubblefield, Pete Tucker.

SOLDIERS: George Anderson, R. R. Boyd, James Carpenter, Robert Jennings, Robert E. Lewis, Dr. Harold Phalen, Frank Ryland, Walter Sheppe.

INDIANS: James D. Carter, Elliott Miller, Travis Turner.

DIGGERS: Eugene Black, Russell Carlisle, Jule Dews, Wilbert Keys, John Manos, Robert Pace, Rex Sater, Murray Shapiro.

GUARDS: John Turner, Reed Whipple.

WOUNDED SOLDIERS: George Anderson, R. R. Boyd, James Carpenter, Robert Jennings, Robert E. Lewis, Elliott Miller, Dr. Harold Phalen, Frank Ryland, Walter Sheppe.

COURTIERS: Mayer Binder, Shanley Keeter, Nathaniel White.

BRITISH SOLDIERS: Eugene Black, Russell Carlisle, Dr. James D. Carter, Jule Dews, Wilbert Keys, Robert Pace, Rex Sater, Murray Shapiro, Travis Turner, Reed Whipple.

TOWNSPEOPLE OF RICHMOND: Virginia Adair, George Anderson, Clinton Atkinson, Nancy Beamer, Caroline Bell, Virginia Bell, Eugene Black, Marguerite Bozarth, James Bray, Frances Brigham, Russell Carlisle, Jule Dews, Mary Frances Faison, Lore Foltin, Florence Gaither, Clarice Garrison, Mrs. Arthur Gordon, Marie Hunt, Virginia James, Jane Johnson, Shanley Keeter, Wilbert Keys, Ronald King, William Larner, Kenneth Lassiter, Mrs. Ernest J. Lee, Kenneth McGinn, Elliott

Miller, Robert Pace, Virginia Parthenis, Grace Raiter, Sherry Roberts, Margaret Rudd, Murray Shapiro, Margaret Smith, John Turner, Helen Walker, Reed Whipple, June White.

THE SCENES

ACT I

SCENE 1: Prologue.
SCENE 2: London—The Audience Chamber in the Palace of King George the Third, a summer night, 1775.
SCENE 3: A Committee Room in the Capitol at Williamsburg, several months later.
SCENE 4: A house in Philadelphia, June, 1776.
SCENE 5: Robert Gordon's home in Williamsburg, some days later.
SCENE 6: Before the Jail in Williamsburg, sometime later.
SCENE 7: The Palace Green in Williamsburg, the same day.
Intermission: 10 Minutes

ACT II

SCENE 1: A room in Monticello, winter, 1778.
SCENE 2: A room in the Governor's palace in Williamsburg, 1779.
SCENE 3: The ruined Churchyard at Jamestown, a winter night, 1780.
SCENE 4: London—A Council Room in the Palace of George the Third, 1781.
SCENE 5: The Battlefield at Yorktown, October, 1781.

PROGRAM OF THE FIRST SEASON 269

SCENE 6: A farmhouse near Yorktown, a few days later.
SCENE 7: The Bluffs at Richmond, sometime later.

Time: The latter part of the Eighteenth Century.
Place: London, Philadelphia and Virginia.

THE COMMON GLORY CHORUS

SOPRANOS:
  Hortense Brigham
  Jean Farrow
  Jeanne Anne Harrup
  Marianne Lewis-Jones
  Frances McCrary
  Betty Mullinix
  Sally Robeson
  Martha Robinson
  Mary Unruh

TENORS:
  Ollie J. Amon, Jr.
  Ralph Bailey
  Jack B. Hoey
  Edward Hudgins
  George C. Pitts, Jr.
  C. Warren Smith

ALTOS:
  Carol Achenbach
  Helen Hopkins
  Emily Leitner
  Virginia Northcott
  Barbara Seifert
  Caroline Sprouse
  Joan Stout
  Dorothea Thedieck
  Joyce Wilck
  Audrey LeDoyen

BASSES:
  Franklin Bon
  James Boyce
  Joseph W. Brinkley
  Dennis Cogle
  Bill Cooley
  Warren Sprouse
  Fred Tubbs
  Bill Williams

THE COMMON GLORY STAFF

House Manager ....Louis Philhower
Assistant Directors ....Anthony Manzi
                                Howard Scammon

Assistant Technical Director	Bruce Johnson
Sound Engineer	John Daley
Crowdmaster	Robert Jennings
Electrician	Wilford Leach
Assistant Electrician	George Sheehan
Wardrobe Mistress	Rachel Hitchins
Property Assistants	Robert Stevens
	Marjorie Oak
Technical Assistants	David Weiss
	John Dayton
Draftsman	Paul Lipinski
Scenery Construction Staff	Thomas Belvin
	Harvey Chappell
	Jean Cutler
	Warren Galbreath
	Martin Greenwood
	William Jolly
	Robley Miles
	Walter Sheppe
	Eugene White
Costume Staff	Martha Armstrong
	Jane Beale
	Emma Creasy
	Loraine Evans
	Nancy Gordon
	Elizabeth Gilliam
	Mildred Harmon
	Louise Holmes
	Virginia Keller
	Florence Lee
	Susan Norsworthy
	Elizabeth Phalen
	Rebecca Preddy
	Hazel Ryan
	Louise Tucker
	Espie Warburton

Group Leaders in Cast ....Evalyn Blandford
Arthur Livick
Eugene Ninde
Georgia Selph
Reed Whipple
Shanley Keeter
William Larner
Murray Shapiro
Ben Bray
Clinton Atkinson
Kenneth Lassiter
Technical Assistants in Cast ....Eugene Black
Murray Shapiro
Rex Sater
Felix Hoffmann
Ben Bray
Nathaniel White
Shanley Keeter
George Anderson
Make-Up Assistants in Cast ....William Larner
Dick Owen
Marie Hunt
Annabelle Koenig
Felix Hoffmann
Kenneth McGinn
Properties Assistants in Cast........Evalyn Blandford
Bristow Hardin, Jr.
Reed Whipple
Clinton Atkinson
Box Office Staff ....M. W. Foster
J. A. Caldwell
Horace Ridenour
Luther Farinholt
Dixon Foster
Ruth Hodges
Gate Attendants ....Tom Restrick
Robert Griffin
Thomas Athey
F. M. Thompson

272 PROGRAM OF THE FIRST SEASON

Ushers	C. H. Pritcherd
	Richard King
	Charles Dickerson
	Samuel Helfrich
	John O'Neal
	Hal Jackson
	Roy Shelor
	Bobbie Barrett
Programs	Elva Bell Waltrip
	Mary Sue Pitman
	Mary F. Ray
	Martha A. Ray
	Lois Kendrew
	Janet Preddy
	Eva Lindsey
	Sadie Mahone
Parking Attendants	Carlton Buchanan
	Lawrence Dickerson
	Gardiner Brooks
	Louis S. Philhower, Jr.
	Robert Cottingham
	Perry Deal
	Douglas Johnson
	W. G. Tucker
	Douglas Dewing

OFFICERS OF THE JAMESTOWN CORPORATION

Honorary President
HONORABLE WILLIAM M. TUCK
Governor of Virginia

President
COLGATE W. DARDEN, JR.

Secretary
WILLIAM A. WRIGHT

Vice-President
CHANNING M. HALL

Treasurer
SAMUEL H. PLUMMER

PROGRAM OF THE FIRST SEASON

THE BOARD OF TRUSTEES OF THE JAMESTOWN CORPORATION

Thomas J. Allen
General James A. Anderson
George Prince Arnold
Robert C. Atherholt
Miss Ellen Bagby
Herbert A. Claiborne
Paul W. Crockett
Homer L. Ferguson
C. Wiley Grandy

Hattie Belle Gresham
Mrs. Philip W. Hiden
Jack G. Holtzclaw
Albert S. Johnson
W. C. Martin
Robert F. Nelson
Bela W. Norton
Dr. John E. Pomfret
Alexander W. Weddell

For Reservations and Additional Information, Call, Write or Wire

THE JAMESTOWN CORPORATION
Williamsburg, Virginia

www.ingramcontent.com/pod-product-compliance
Lightning Source LLC
Chambersburg PA
CBHW021356290426
44108CB00010B/265